THE BOWNE HOUSE

A National Shrine to Religious Freedom

THE BOWNE HOUSE HISTORICAL SOCIETY
BOWNE STREET AND FOX LANE
FLUSHING, LONG ISLAND

Copyright, 1953
THE BOWNE HOUSE HISTORICAL SOCIETY

BENJ. H. TYRREL
PRINTERS
110 Greenwich St., N.Y.

Contents

	PAGE
Officers of The Bowne House Historical Society	4
Trustees of The Bowne House Historical Society	4
The President's Message—Hon. Charles S. Colden	5
Freedom's Way—Dr. Albert B. Corey	7
John Bowne and Freedom of Religion—Haynes Trébor	9
The Flushing Remonstrance—December 27, 1657	20–21
Interior and Furnishings of Bowne House	22
The Bowne House Historical Society—Miss Margaret I. Carman	26
An Appreciation	35
Committees of The Bowne House Historical Society	36
Membership in The Bowne House Historical Society	38
Life Members	39
Sustaining Members	41
Regular Members	42

OFFICERS

OF

THE BOWNE HOUSE HISTORICAL SOCIETY

Honorable Charles S. Colden .... *President*

LeRoy T. Stratton .... *Vice President*

Laurence B. Halleran .... *Vice President*

Franklin F. Regan .... *Treasurer*

Mrs. Edward J. Streator .... *Secretary*

Miss Margaret I. Carman .... *Historian*

TRUSTEES OF THE BOWNE HOUSE HISTORICAL SOCIETY

Max Abramson	1945-	Samuel D. Jones	1945-
Dr. Charles H. Campbell	1946-	Dr. George J. Lawrence	1945-1949*
Miss Margaret I. Carman	1952-	Miss Mary MacLeod	1947-
Honorable Charles S. Colden	1945-	Rabbi Max Meyer	1945-
Harry L. Dayton	1945-	Miss Anna M. O'Connor	1946-
Sherman S. Ely	1947-1948	Harold G. Parker	1945-1949*
Mrs. Paul B. Findley	1945-	William Bowne Parsons	1945-
W. Flemer Foulk	1946-	Charles U. Powell	1945-
Reverend B. A. Galloway	1945-1948	Franklin F. Regan	1946-
Arthur H. Greeley	1946-1947	LeRoy T. Stratton	1945-1952
Rev. Dr. Norman A. Hall	1945-	Mrs. Edward J. Streator	1945-
John J. Halleran	1945-	Mrs. John H. Tennent	1947-
Laurence B. Halleran	1947-	Haynes Trébor	1945-
Mrs. Laurence B. Halleran	1946-	William H. Waechter	1946-
Douglas G. Hardgrove	1945-	Mrs. Charles B. Williams	1946-1949
Gale Hunter	1945-	Very Reverend Monsignor John D. Wynne	1945-

* Deceased.

The President's Message

THIS nation was settled by men and women in search of freedom they could not find elsewhere. Strong in their convictions, they knew that God moved in all the affairs of man, and, therefore, they fought, from the early beginnings, to establish "liberty of conscience."

Nowhere in our land did this ideal find greater practical expression than in the old Town of Flushing, whose Charter, issued in October, 1645, guaranteed to all "the right to have and enjoy liberty of conscience." Its early inhabitants resisted, with great courage and sacrifice, all efforts to suppress religious liberty, insisting upon accepting people of every faith into their community.

It was in Flushing, in 1657, that one of the significant documents in the struggle for religious liberty in America was issued—The Flushing Remonstrance—protesting Peter Stuyvesant's ban on Quakers and the practice of their religion in the Town. Of this great document, the distinguished American Historian, John Fiske, has said:

> "The names of thirty-one valiant men are signed to this document. I do not know whether Flushing has ever raised a fitting monument to their memory. If I could have my way, I would have the protest carved on a stately obelisk, with the name of Edward Heart, Town Clerk, and the thirty other Dutch and English names appended, and would have it set up where all might read it for the glory of the Town that had such men for its founders."

While no "stately obelisk" has been erected, men and women of vision have, in the establishment of Bowne House as a National Shrine to Religious Freedom, raised a fitting memorial to those who so valiantly strove for liberty of conscience. It was to that old house—built in 1661—that John Bowne invited Quakers to hold services. Rather than obey the mandate of the Governor and the Council to abstain from Quaker meetings, under penalty of fine and banishment to the Old World, Bowne suffered solitary dungeon confinement until set free in Holland, upon his earnest plea for tolerance and freedom for all people to worship God according to their lights, and their different beliefs.

Nearly a thousand of the good people of our community gave generously of their time, their substance and their enthusiastic devotion to bring about the successful tercentenary celebration of the granting of the Charter to the Town of Flushing, culminating in the dedication of Bowne House on October 10, 1945, as a National Shrine to Religious Freedom. I wish it were possible here to name all of them, but the necessary limitations of space and more important, the fear that even one name should be missing from the record, precludes the attempt. The roll of members of the Bowne House Historical Society contains many of those who have participated in our common cause.

As was so eloquently said on another occasion by our fellow member, The Honorable Charles W. Froessel, Associate Judge of the Court of Appeals of the State of New York: "Important events of the moment are too readily forgotten. The scattered records of today so often fall into oblivion tomorrow. To rebuild happenings of any given period requires endless research among failing recollections and disbursed memoranda."

Through this little book, compiled under the direction of our Bowne House Book Committee, an effort has been made to preserve the Bowne House story. The articles by Mr. Haynes Trébor, Bowne House Trustee, an author and Long Island Historian of distinction, Miss Margaret I. Carman, Trustee and Historian of the Society, and Dr. Albert B. Corey, New York State Historian, have captured and beautifully expressed the spirit for which our beloved Bowne House stands. To them and to our fellow member, Mr. Samuel S. Tripp, author, lecturer, and distinguished past president of the Queens County Bar Association, who has given devoted assistance to us in editing this book during many days and nights of preparation, we are all most grateful.

As the years pass along and we observe the ever-widening sphere of the beneficent influence of Bowne House and realize the magnificent contributions made to its cause by so many patriotic and devoted men and women, I, with deep humility, offer to each of them my thanks for the rich privilege which they have granted me in working with them in this noble cause.

CHARLES S. COLDEN, *President.*

THE BOWNE HOUSE—A view from the garden showing the original portion containing the kitchen in which religious meetings of Quakers were held in defiance of Governor Stuyvesant's Edict against that sect.

Freedom's Way

ALBERT B. COREY*

MR. TRÉBOR's delightful and penetrating story of *John Bowne and the Freedom of Religion* gives full meaning to the statement that "good history is both an index of liberty and a bulwark in its defense." It is the more welcome because it is published appropriately at a moment characterized by Mr. Justice Douglas as a period when the pulse beat of freedom is more feeble than at any other time in the history of the United States. It is an age-old story which must never grow old in the telling. Like freedom itself, its story must remain ever fresh and new, challenging a deeper devotion to it by all our people.

John Bowne's story contains all of the elements which have characterized the fight for freedom in the western world. It is essentially a demand for freedom of conscience; that is, the right of a man to exercise and use his own judgment. It is a refusal to be herded into acceptance of mass thinking or coercion by the governing authorities in matters touching his religious faith which his conscience cannot approve. It is recognition that a man's conscience must be his guide lest, becoming the slave of external pressures, he finds he is no longer free.

The struggle to attain freedom of conscience has been associated with the struggle to attain other freedoms, notably freedom of association which is basic to all others and without which they cannot flourish. For what freedom does a man have who is prohibited from joining with others to propagate a faith common to them all? Of all the rights guaranteed by the Bill of Rights in our federal and state constitutions, it has been said appropriately that freedom of association "is the very essence of liberty. Without it no other liberty can have very much content."

Whether John Bowne understood these issues as they have been stated here is immaterial. The fact is that he fought for freedom to believe as he chose and freedom of a new sect, the Quakers, to worship together. It is understandable why the opposition to the Quakers was so sharp. Despite changes brought about by the Reformation there was still everywhere in Europe a strong tendency toward requiring conformity to state religions. Puritans in Massachusetts while demanding freedom of conscience and association for themselves denounced those who did not agree with them and, in some instances, forced them to flee. The Quakers, moreover, were a militant and troublesome people who sometimes refused to obey the civil authorities and were frequently objectionable to their neighbors. It is little wonder that dissenters from the established patterns of religious thought, and sometimes of political thought as well, were merely permitted by the public authorities to meet together. Toleration of this kind meant that they were at the mercy of those who allowed them to worship in their own way merely as a privilege, not as a right.

Freedom is established through the action of individuals, acting singly or in small groups, who are willing to suffer every kind of pain and penalty in

---

*DR. ALBERT BICKMORE COREY is a distinguished scholar and historian in the field of modern history and government. Born in Madras, India, of missionary parents, he attended high school in Bangalore, subsequently moving to Canada to live. From 1916 to 1918, he served in the first World War as a corporal in the Canadian Infantry and as a pilot officer in the R. A. F. in France from 1918 to 1919. His A.B. came from Acadia in Nova Scotia in 1922 and the degree of A.M. from both Harvard and Toronto Universities in 1923 and 1934 respectively. His Ph.D. was awarded by Clark University in 1934. From the time of his appointment to the faculty of Waynesburg College in Pennsylvania in 1925, he has had a full teaching career. He was named head of the department of history and government at St. Lawrence University two years later. Distinguished fellowships were awarded him by Toronto and Clark and he was lecturer at Queen's University, Kingston, Ontario in the summer of 1937.

A special interest in international questions was shown by his work as originator and organizer of the biennial conferences of Canadian-American affairs held jointly by St. Lawrence and Queen's Universities under the auspices of the Carnegie Endowment for International Peace, his authorship of the book, *The Crisis of 1830-1842 in Canadian-American Relations*, published in 1941, and his editing of the *Proceedings of the Canadian-American Conferences* in various years.

In 1944 Dr. Corey was named New York State Historian, an office which his broad interests and administrative ability have enabled him to conduct with distinction. He is currently the President of the American Association for State and Local History.

pursuit of their objective. So it was with those who signed the Flushing Remonstrance, and so it was with John Bowne. Their concept of liberty is that which has come to prevail in the United States; it is "liberty within the law," wherein each has the same rights as his neighbor. It is the concept of civil rights, defined by Governor John Winthrop of Massachusetts Bay in his *Journal* in 1645, as "a liberty to do that which is good, just, and honest," thereby excluding "a liberty to evil as well as to good," which, is license and hence "incompatible and inconsistent with authority." It is a concept which deals with concrete matters like freedom of assembly, religion, speech, and the press. But here is the rub. Laws are interpreted and enforced by men. It is important to recognize, therefore, that these constitutional rights are only safeguarded by the good sense of public officials, public opinion, and the ballot box.

Too much emphasis cannot be placed upon the need for safeguarding the rights of the individual, for in democratic society he is and remains its key. Constitutional government exists to protect and promote his welfare. The history of the recognition of the importance of the individual is very long. Suffice it to say that by the seventeenth century freedom for the individual meant freedom of worship. It was won in the face of exclusion by Puritans in New England of all but their own adherents from the practice of their faith, as well as from participation in civil government. It was won elsewhere in the face of opposition to various religious groups. It has been safeguarded by constitutional enactment which separates church and state. It will remain intact if the spirit of the constitution is honestly and generously carried into execution by the adherents of every creed.

There are those today who deny that "the best test of truth is the power of the thought to get itself accepted in the competition of the market," or as Milton put it "who ever knew truth put to the worse in a free and open encounter?" An unreasoning hysteria is gripping the country threatening the liberties guaranteed by the Bill of Rights. Men are under attack for speaking and writing honestly about the convictions they hold. Their words are taken out of context, their motives are attacked, their characters are besmirched.

It must be driven home again and again that "our freedom is our security." Any denial of the guarantees of the first ten amendments is, as President Truman said when dedicating the newly enshrined Declaration of Independence, Constitution, and Bill of Rights, "worse than dangerous, it is absolutely fatal to liberty. The eternal threat to liberty should not drive us into suppressing liberty at home."

Judge Colden and his associates deserve the highest commendation for preserving the Bowne House and establishing it as a shrine to religious freedom for all of the American people. It is a fine old house, beautifully restored and furnished as it might well have been in John Bowne's day. Governed and operated by men and women of every faith and creed, working harmoniously together, it exemplifies as no other house the spirit of complete freedom of conscience. This is the reason for its existence. This is its glory.

"Religious freedom is guaranteed to each one of us by the Constitution of the United States, and he who would persecute, embarrass or discriminate against any man because of his religious faith and worship violates our fundamental law. Hold yourselves everywhere and always above and apart from class hatred, and above and apart from religious persecution."—*Nicholas Murray Butler.*

John Bowne and Freedom of Religion

HAYNES TRÉBOR*

IN the establishment of religious freedom in America John Bowne ranks in importance with John Peter Zenger in the establishment of freedom of the press.** Both played leading parts in the formation of the basic concepts of liberty which later were incorporated into our Bill of Rights. Bowne, however, accomplished his mission in a community which itself contributed more to religious freedom than any other in America—Flushing, New York.

John Bowne was born in Derbyshire, England, in 1627. At the age of 22 he migrated to Massachusetts with his father and sister. The family came to Flushing in 1651, but John soon returned to Massachusetts where he prospered as a merchant. Three years later, however, he settled permanently in

Old print of Bowne House from Phelps Stokes Collection in the New York Public Library.

The Bowne House Today.

Flushing where he became a farmer. In 1656 he was married to Hannah Feake. Tramping through the surrounding woodland with his wife, Bowne personally selected the trees from which timbers were hand-hewn to build their home. So well was it constructed that today the original portion of the Bowne House, the kitchen, with bedrooms upstairs, is little different from what it was in 1661 when the house was built.

---

* The author of this article is a member of the Board of Trustees of The Bowne House Historical Society and the Executive Secretary of the Flushing Chamber of Commerce. He has been a life-long student of the history of Flushing and of Long Island generally.

** John Peter Zenger, the publisher of the New York Weekly Journal, exposed in 1733 corruption and tyranny in the Colonial Government of New York. For this he was imprisoned for nine months, following which he was tried on charges of "scandalous, malicious, false and seditious reflection." His attorney, eighty year-old Andrew Hamilton, contended that there could be no libel if what Zenger published was the truth. The unanimous verdict of the jury, acquitting the defendant, established the principle of freedom of the press in America.

FRIENDS MEETING HOUSE, Northern Boulevard, east of Main Street, Flushing. The Quakers of Flushing, who for 30 years had met in the Bowne House, purchased this site in 1692 and first services were held in 1694 when the building was completed; it was enlarged to its present size in 1719.

IN 1662 John Bowne defied Governor Peter Stuyvesant's Edict against Quakers by permitting that sect to conduct religious meetings in his home. As a result, he suffered arrest and banishment until released after a trial in Holland by a committee of the Amsterdam Chamber of the Dutch West India Company. He then returned to his home in Flushing where the Quakers continued to worship for thirty years until the Friends Meeting House, which is still used for regular religious worship, was completed in 1694.

It is this old home of John Bowne, located on Bowne Street and Fox Lane in Flushing, Long Island, which in 1945 became a national shrine to religious freedom after its acquisition for that purpose by the Bowne House Historical Society, and which was conceived and founded during the Tercentenary Celebration of Flushing that year.

ON October 10, 1645, William Kieft, Governor of the Dutch Province of New Netherland, issued a charter to a group of Englishmen to found the Town of Flushing. They were promised "the right to have and enjoy liberty of conscience." They and their descendants and other men of "divers views" on religion who followed them, courageously resisted every attempt to infringe upon that right, accepting in their community people of every faith and belief. Their attitude was eloquently expressed in the Flushing Remonstrance nearly three hundred years ago, the principles of which are identical with those contained in the first article of the Bill of Rights, now a fundamental part of our American heritage: "Congress shall make no law respecting the establishment of religion or prohibiting the free exercise thereof."

Undoubtedly the first declaration of religious tolerance by any group of ordinary citizens in American history, motivated solely by the consciences of free men, the Remonstrance was unique in that, at a time when it was unpopular, and unlaw-

THE BUILDING has been in continuous use as a place of worship since it was erected, except during the Revolution, when it was used by the British Army for a prison and barracks. The original benches were broken by the British soldiers and used as firewood and those now in use were installed after the Revolution.

"SHIP'S KNEES," carved out, usually from an oak tree following the natural contour of trunk and limb, were used in early sailing ships to brace the deck to the hull. In the Quaker Meeting House in Flushing, they were used as shown in the photograph to brace the heavy beams on the upper floor.

LIBERTY of conscience became a popular and frequently used phrase in the middle of the 17th Century, more often than not with a selfish motive. It was a handy slogan for the promoters of colonial ventures. It was subject to a variety of interpretations that might even justify its application under conditions of rampant bigotry, prejudice and intolerance. At best, it rarely went further than to cover persons professing the Christian faith—and in some places it was a punishable offense to recognize Catholics as Christians.

Yet the Puritan could argue convincingly that the New England colonies had "liberty of conscience." Some of their founders came to America for that purpose—to obtain liberty of conscience for themselves. Members of other sects might, and did, live there without undue molestation, provided they paid taxes, helped support the established church, were discreet in their behavior and refrained from public expression of their religious and political beliefs. The whipping post, the gallows and banishment were merely deterrents for those who, like the Quakers, Anabaptists and a few other militant sects, insisted upon openly practicing their forms of worship, or challenging the doctrines of the orthodox clergy and the synonymous authority of church and state.

The Cavaliers of Virginia, who also enjoyed liberty of conscience, laid penalties on all who might dissent from the Anglican church and required conformity to the Book of Common Prayer. Yet a fairly large group of Puritans, and others, managed to exist in the colony.

In only two of the colonies, Rhode Island and Maryland, was there any semblance of true religious freedom. This had been brought about almost entirely by two men, Roger Williams and Lord Baltimore, rather than by popular sentiment.

Maryland was successfully founded upon a basis of tolerance through the honest desire of Lord Baltimore to erect a colony where Protestants and Roman Catholics might live on terms of equality, amity and

ful, to respect the rights and opinions of others in matters of religion, effective use was made of public opinion to check the arbitrary use of governmental power to suppress basic human freedom.

Incensed by a ban ordered by Governor Peter Stuyvesant in 1657 on the harboring of Quakers newly arrived in the colony, or the holding of religious services by this sect, twenty-eight freeholders of the Town of Flushing proclaimed that not only would they welcome Quakers to their town and homes, but any "sons of Adam who come in love among us" and would not "condemn, punish, banish, persecute or lay violent hands upon anyone, in whatever name, form or title he might appear."

Dismissal of town officials, fines and imprisonment and threats of banishment failed to suppress this remarkable spirit of tolerance. Flushing continued to be a haven for Quakers, although they were forced to hold meetings secretly in the woods to escape persecution by the New Netherland authorities. Nowhere in colonial America was a more consistent and valiant effort made to establish true religious freedom. The Remonstrance was only one of several instances in which its people fought for the right of every man to worship God in his own way.

forbearance. The famous "Act Concerning Religion," adopted by the Maryland Assembly in 1649, appears to have been drafted by Lord Baltimore himself. This was a formal declaration of tolerance of one religious body by another, but did not guarantee full religious freedom. While it proclaimed religious tolerance, it protected only the Trinitarians. Among others, it excluded Jews, who consequently avoided Maryland during its entire colonial period.

JUDGED by the standards of the times, Rhode Island was the only colony offering actual religious freedom. As in the case of Maryland, this was due to the personal convictions of one man and was the effect rather than the cause in the founding of the colony. When he was banished from Massachusetts, where his ideas on theology and government differed radically from those of the Puritan state, it had not been Roger Williams' intention to create a haven either for religious or political refugees, but to do missionary work among the Indians. It was only after others had joined him in forming a settlement at Providence, and some form of government was necessary, that Williams drew up an agreement, in the form of a social compact, whereby the inhabitants were to subject themselves in active or passive obedience to such orders and understandings as should be the will of the greater number of the householders. Later he added the phrase, "only in Civil matters."

Subsequently, in distributing lands which he had purchased from the Indians, Roger Williams laid down the rule that there was to be equality of shares and recognition of the fact that the place was "for those who were destitute especially for conscience's sake." Thus was established the principle of religious liberty which became fixed in the life of the plantation. Advocating the complete separation of church and state, Williams opposed the absolute authority of any one church. In his "True Picture of a Commonwealth," written in 1655, he included Papists, Protestants, Jews and Turks, all of whom he thought to have a right not only to be tolerated, but to live and worship in their own way. He would grant liberty even to "seducing teachers," who, whether pagan, Jewish or anti-Christian, might still be obedient subjects to the civil laws.

While he stood for complete equality as far as liberty of conscience was concerned, Williams nevertheless was always ready to enter into arguments on theological questions. He disagreed with some of his associates in Rhode Island, and engaged in a spirited debate with the Quakers. A pamphlet which he issued, titled "George Fox Digg'd Out of His Burrowes," was termed by the Quaker leader "a very wicked and envious book . . . written against the truth and the Friends."

IN attempting to effectuate their views on religious tolerance the people of Flushing were confronted with a vastly different problem than were those of Maryland or Rhode Island. It was not possible for them merely to subscribe to and support an established policy of "liberty of conscience." It became necessary for them to challenge the authority of a government under which they lived as aliens, and to which they were beholden for the land on which they made their homes. They were subject to laws and regulations not of their own making and had no voice either in the administration of the colony or the enforcement of its laws. It therefore required a high degree of courage and audacity for the people of Flushing to demand that the government extend to all others the liberties which they had been given, and openly declare their defiance of a law directed, not at themselves, but at a newly arrived group whose religious beliefs were, at the time, different from their own.

The charter granted by Governor Kieft to establish a town at Flushing was probably the most liberal arrangement for any settlement in America up to that time. For the first time, the right was given "to have and enjoy liberty of conscience, according to the custom and manner of Holland, without molestation or disturbance from any magistrates, or any other ecclesiastical minister, that may pretend jurisdiction over them."

While liberty of conscience in the manner and custom of Holland did not imply religious freedom, in the modern sense, Holland, along with the Turkish Empire, had the most liberal attitude toward religious tolerance of any of the European nations. The Reformed church was the only officially recognized church and everyone was taxed to support it, but from early in the 17th Century, Protestants of all sects enjoyed political rights and, in most instances, privileges of public worship. Catholics were permitted to have their own places of worship if the exteriors were built to look like houses. Jews had no rights, but were granted asylum and could worship privately in peace.

Whether the provision for "liberty of conscience" was inserted in the Flushing patent as a generous gesture on the part of Governor Kieft in his eagerness to obtain additional settlers into the colony and establish new towns which might serve as buffers to Indian attacks on New Amsterdam, or whether it was the result of shrewd negotiating by the leaders of the group, is not known. There is some reason to assume the latter. The fact remains, however, that the patent seemed to assure the Flushing settlers, for themselves and their heirs, the privilege of self-determination in matters of religion without interference by the authorities of either church or state. In any event, it was so interpreted by the settlers who staunchly fought against any infringement of that right.

From the very beginning Flushing would have no established church. Governor Stuyvesant tried to force the town to accept as its minister the Reverend Francis Doughty of Maspeth, whom the Dutch clergy considered in agreement with the Reformed church. Some of the citizens approved this action but many others did not wish to attend the services and refused to be taxed for the minister's support, despite threats of prosecution by the provincial Council.

IT was not until 1652, after Stuyvesant had been governor for several years, that serious interference with worship by other than the Reformed sect began. Stuyvesant, himself a strict Calvinist, is sometimes accused of having started religious persecution on his own, although it appears more likely that the Dutch clergy had begun to exert pressure to check the spread of other doctrines in the colony. Many of the laity, both English and Dutch, were only too eager to support and encourage a policy of intolerance.

The Holland government meanwhile was advertising hospitality to persons "of tender conscience in England and elsewhere oppressed." Mindful that its liberal policy had once saved the colony from veritable bankruptcy and was now paying dividends in its rapid growth and development, the government did not wish to deal harshly with any elements in the population, which now contained such a mixture of nationalities that it was necessary to translate all official notices into three languages. At the same time it felt that some restrictions were necessary because many of these alien groups, especially the English, were trying to obtain special commercial and trading privileges in competition with the Dutch. They also were agitating for political representation in the tightly controlled management of the colony.

With the ecclesiastical authorities in Holland supporting the provincial clergy in their complaints of the increase in unorthodox sects, the government temporized and sanctioned rigorous enforcement of laws restricting religious tolerance which long had been a dead letter at home. The West India Company, while mildly reprimanding Stuyvesant on occasion for being overly vehement, also hesitated to take a firm stand against persecution.

When a group of Lutherans asked permission to call a clergyman of their own, Stuyvesant told them he was bound by his oath of office to sanction only the established church of Holland and imprisoned some leaders of the group for attempting to hold services. For this he was mildly rebuked by the directors of the Amsterdam Chamber of the Company, which had supervision over the administration of the colony. They informed him that they "would have been better pleased if you had not published the placard against the Lutherans and committed them to prison, as it has always been our intention to treat them kind and lenient." He was advised not to continue this or any similar practice without the knowledge of the company's directors and to let the Lutherans have "free liberties exercised in their houses." Nevertheless a Lutheran minister was later arrested for conducting public worship and banished from the colony.

IN 1656 William Wickenden, an itinerant cobbler, came to Flushing from Rhode Island. A Baptist, Wickenden declared he had "a commission from Christ" and began preaching his doctrine in the town, baptising a number of converts in the river. The people of Flushing showed no inclination to interfere with Wickenden's activities and Sheriff William Hallett even permitted him to hold services in his home. As soon as he heard about this, Stuyvesant removed Hallett from office and fined him. Wickenden, whom the governor described as "a troublesome fellow," was shipped back to Rhode Island.

Meanwhile the arrival of Quakers in New Netherland added fuel to the flames of religious controversy and set off a new and more violent wave of intolerance and persecution. The Society of Friends, started in England by George Fox in 1645, the same year that Flushing was founded, was a militantly evangelistic sect which seemed to delight in making martyrs of themselves and which used every opportunity to expound their particular doctrines, even to the extent of entering the churches of other denominations and debating with the ministers in the midst of service.

The first Quakers who had gone to New England in 1656 had been ordered to desist in their preaching or leave the colonies. Those who refused were taken to the gallows. Determined to defy this persecution, a group of Quakers, led by the Reverend Robert Hodgson, had set out from England for Boston. Their ship was blown off its course and they landed in New Amsterdam instead. Two women in the group immediately began "preaching turbulently in the streets of New Amsterdam," declaring that the day of judgment was at hand and calling upon all people to repent. They were dragged off to prison.

Hodgson went to the English settlements on Long Island to preach. At the invitation of Lady Moody, he spoke at Gravesend and then made his way to Hempstead. There he was arrested by the pious English magistrates for attempting to hold services out of doors on the Sabbath and turned over to the Dutch authorities who forced him to walk back to New Amsterdam chained to the tail of a cart. The Council condemned him to pay a heavy fine or work for two years shackled to the slaves of the West India Company. This punishment not being enough, Hodgson was flogged until Stuyvesant's sister pleaded to spare his life and was then deported to Rhode Island.

More Quakers came into the province and some of the inhabitants of the English towns were showing them hospitality and even attending surreptitious meetings. Enraged by these activities, Stuyvesant decided upon vigorous measures. Henry Townsend was arrested and fined for holding a meeting in his house in Jamaica. The Governor then issued a proclamation, which was printed on placards and posted in every town, declaring that any person entertaining a Quaker for a single night was to be fined fifty florins, of which one half was to go to whoever informed the authorities, and that vessels bringing any Quaker into the province would be confiscated.

THE reading of the Governor's placard must have been greeted with angry comments among the townspeople of Flushing. The new ordinance was probably discussed in the homes and wherever men met in the town. Sentiment grew to oppose this

new infringement upon the right to enjoy liberty of conscience as provided in the town charter. It was decided to send a remonstrance to the governor in protest of his action. A remonstrance was the customary instrument among the Dutch for expression of public opinion. Holland had always respected public opinion, and the unorganized, unofficially expressed opinion of its people had been a strong force in liberalizing the government of that nation. Remonstrances were frequently used in New Netherland, either as a petition to the government or the West India Company for special privileges or as a protest of grievances.

To Town Clerk Edward Heart fell the task of preparing such a document. When it was ready, the Remonstrance was read and approved at a town meeting held in the home of Michael Milner on December 27, 1657. It covered two sheets of paper, at the bottom of which was the notation: "Written by me, Edward Heart, clericus." On the top of a third sheet Sheriff Tobias Feake boldly signed his name. Magistrate William Noble and others attending the town meeting added their signatures. During the next two days Magistrate Edward Farrington and several freeholders not present at the meeting, along with two from Jamaica, put their names to the document. Then, on December 29, Sheriff Feake journeyed to New Amsterdam and handed the document to Governor Stuyvesant at a meeting of the Council. The Governor angrily ordered Feake imprisoned and during a stormy session of the Council warrants were issued for the arrest also of Heart and the two magistrates.

Ironically, at the same session of the Council at which the Flushing Remonstrance was presented, complaint was received from certain "principal inhabitants" of Jamaica that their fellow citizen, Henry Townsend, one of the signers of the Remonstrance, was again harboring Quakers, despite his arrest four months previously on the same charge. The Council ordered Townsend held until he paid a fine of three hundred florins. It is not known whether the complainants against Townsend received their half of the fine for informing on him.

Edward Heart was subjected to a searching examination with a view of determining the instigator of the Remonstrance. Stuyvesant could not conceive that the people themselves would be moved to tolerance. There had to be a culprit, and Stuyvesant suspected Feake. It is very likely that the Sheriff may have been a prime leader in this affair. Despite prolonged questioning, Heart stoutly maintained that the Remonstrance contained only what were the sentiments of all the people, as he had gathered them "from the general votes of the inhabitants," and that it had been signed willingly, following action taken at the town meeting. When nothing of importance could be extracted from him, Heart was sent to prison.

After three weeks' confinement, Heart's neighbors interceded in his behalf, since he was elderly, with a large family to support. He was released from prison, but not until he had been made to apologize for having "written a writing whereat you (the Governor) take offense" and pleaded with Stuyvesant "for your mercy, not your judgment." The two magistrates who had signed the Remonstrance, defended their action by declaring that "our patent grants us liberty of conscience" and that the Remonstrance, as a petition to the governor, was "honest in intent." Upon repenting that they had "acted so inconsiderately" and promising "to offend no more in that kind," they too were released, but were suspended from office.

IT is perhaps significant that Stuyvesant directed his ire over the Remonstrance chiefly at the town officials, and so far as the records of the time show, the other signers were not punished, as individuals. Perhaps Stuyvesant was just as much concerned over the political implications of the town's actions in this case as he was of the religious issues involved.

In fairness to Stuyvesant, it should be borne in mind that he had his problems with the English who settled the western end of Long Island, the area which later became the County of Queens. Four years before, the people of Flushing had been among the principal agitators of a protest over taxation without representation for the English towns in the New Netherland government. Tobias Feake had been chosen as Flushing's representative to a provincial diet or land-dag, the first of its kind in America, which was the outgrowth of this agitation and which drafted a remonstrance sharply criticizing Stuyvesant's arbitrary rule.

Small wonder then that Stuyvesant felt that he had to take firm measures against the officials of Flushing for having been parties to the Remonstrance against his ban on the Quakers. That they were sincere in their advocacy of tolerance and acted within the rights and privileges purportedly guaranteed in their town patent was quite beside the point. The fact is that the Quakers were the source of the trouble. As an official, he found in their noisy self-assertion, and the readiness of the English not only to give them asylum but encourage their activities, a threat to his prestige and authority which he hardly could ignore.

Whether the severity of the measures he took in regard to the Flushing Remonstrance was motivated,

in part at least, by political considerations, Stuyvesant was determined that this "new and unheard of heresy" would not occur again in the town of Flushing. While he magnanimously "forgave" the town for its mutinous conduct, he announced that in the future he would appoint a sheriff without nominations from the citizens, as had been the custom, and he would choose a man "acquainted with practical Dutch law." To make sure that his own appointee and the magistrates would not be led astray, the Governor also decreed that there should be chosen "seven of the most reasonable and respectable inhabitants, to be called tribunes or townsmen, and with whom the Sheriff and magistrates shall consult at all times."

But Stuyvesant was unable to subdue the spirit of tolerance. Town Clerk Edward Heart had spoken the truth when he said that the Remonstrance expressed the sentiments of all the people. The officials may have, under duress, been forced to an admission of wrong-doing but the Remonstrance, formally approved at a town meeting and subscribed to by most of the freeholders of the town, was never revoked by any similar action. Quakers continued to find hospitality in Flushing, even though the governor posted his placards warning against harboring them or attending their meetings and quartered troops in nearby Jamaica to apprehend members of the sect and those who dared befriend them.

FEW of the men who gathered before the smoldering fire in the kitchen of Michael Milner's home on the 27th day of December, 1657, and debated an action which held certain peril to each of them, possessed even the rudimentary education to have prepared such "a writing." Some had to sign the document with a crude mark, while the faltering signatures of others were so illegible that their very identity has not been determined with certainty. The men who signed the Remonstrance did not enjoy positions of influence; they were not men of power or wealth; they were humble men whose worldly possessions were a few "morgens" of land from which, by long and arduous labor, they obtained the barest necessities of life for themselves and their families. Their homes, in almost every instance, were the most modest shelters, some of them consisting of no more than a hole dug in the ground and covered by a thatch roof.

But no one, whether Christian, Jew or heathen, would be denied a welcome and God's blessing.

Because the Remonstrance ostensibly concerned only this obscure little settlement and represented the views of a handful of men, most of whose names appear nowhere else in the record of the time, historians have generally neglected to emphasize its importance in the evolution of democracy in the New World. Without parallel anywhere in America, the Flushing Remonstrance had greater significance and its effect was farther reaching than the brief tempest in the Council of the Province of New Netherland might indicate.

THE climax to the wave of religious persecution in New Netherland came in 1662, shortly after John Bowne built his new home in Flushing and invited the Quakers to worship there. For some time the Quakers, to avoid arrest by Stuyvesant's soldiers, had been holding secret meetings in the woods near Flushing. A number of people of the town attended these services and became converts. Among these were John Bowne and his wife, Hannah, who was a stepdaughter of William Hallett, deposed from his office as sheriff in the Wickenden episode.

Complaint quickly went to Governor Stuyvesant from the magistrates of Jamaica that "many of their village were adherents and followers of the abominable Quaker sect and that a large meeting was held at the house of John Bowne in Flushing

every Sunday." Accompanied by a squad of soldiers and armed with an order from the Governor directing all magistrates and inhabitants of English towns to assist him in imprisoning all such persons found in a prohibited or unlawful meeting, an officer was sent to arrest John Bowne. Leaving his wife and two children critically ill, Bowne was taken to New Amsterdam. The Council found him guilty of providing lodgings for some of the "heretical Quakers" and permitting their meetings in his house "in contempt of our order and placards." For these "transactions of the most dangerous consequences," Bowne was ordered to pay a fine of one hundred and fifty florins "with the express warning to abstain himself in future from all such conventicles and meetings." A second offense would bring double the fine and a further violation would mean banishment from the province.

Characteristic of most Quakers of his time, John Bowne stood steadfast in the face of persecution. He would neither pay the fine nor promise to abstain himself from religious services of the Quakers. Bowne was put in solitary confinement in the fort's dungeon, on a diet of coarse bread and water, to think things over.

That failed to have any effect, so the Governor had him moved to a room in the Stadt Huis and the door of his cell was often left unlocked. By allowing Bowne's wife and friends to visit him, Stuyvesant thought Bowne might be persuaded to

change his mind. He was even allowed three days in which to visit his home in Flushing, unescorted, possibly with the hope that he might be tempted to flee the colony. To the astonishment of his jailer, Bowne returned before the time had expired and asked to be locked up. Stuyvesant then let it be known, through some of the minor officials and an English minister, that if Bowne would pay the fine or agree to remove himself from the jurisdiction of the province the whole matter could be forgotten. But Bowne continued to be "obstinate and pervicatious"; so, after three months' imprisonment, it was decided to deport him on the first ship ready to sail "as an example to others." When the ship "Fox" was preparing to depart for Holland, Bowne was offered one last chance to obey the sentence, which he rejected, and was ordered put aboard. At Bowne's request for "something in writing" to explain his crime, Governor Stuyvesant drafted a letter to the directors of the West India Company and dispatched it on the same ship.

AFTER a stormy voyage, the "Fox" put in at Dublin. There Bowne left the ship to journey to England to enlist the help of friends in presenting his case before the Amsterdam Chamber of the company. Since Stuyvesant had made no arrangement to pay for his passage, and Bowne refused to bear the expense of his own banishment, the master of the "Fox" confiscated the chest containing Bowne's personal belongings.

The "Fox" continued to Holland, where Stuyvesant's letter concerning Bowne was delivered. Alarmed when it learned that Stuyvesant, because of his trouble with Bowne, had embarked upon a policy of chasing settlers from the colony and threatened even more severe treatment of other religious offenders, the Amsterdam Chamber dispatched a prompt reply:

"Your Last Letter informed us that you had banished from the Province and sent hither by ship a certain Quaker, *John Bowne* by name: although we heartily desire, that these and other sectarians were not found there, yet as contrary is the case we doubt very much if rigorous proceedings against them can be continued without diminishing the population and stopping immigration, which at so tender an age of the new country, must be promoted by every possible means.

"Wherefore, in this case some connivance should be made at least, and in all events people's conscience should not be forced by anyone but remain free in itself, as long as he is modest and behaves in a lawful manner and therefore does not disturb others or oppose the government.

"And as this maxim of moderation has always been observed by the government of this city which consequently has often had a considerable influx of people, we doubt not that your Province will find this practice beneficial also. You will therefore regulate yourself accordingly."

The question of John Bowne's banishment, however, still remained to be settled. Obtaining a letter of introduction to a Quaker cheesemonger in Amsterdam who would serve as his adviser and interpreter, Bowne made his way to Holland. There the Amsterdam Chamber of the Company, in which the States General was represented, named a committee to hear Bowne's case. This committee showed no hostility over the fact that Bowne was a Quaker, and Bowne was impressed that no objection was made to his wearing his hat, according to the Quaker custom, in the committee's presence. This was quite contrary to his experience in the Council of New Amsterdam, where Stuyvesant had ordered the soldiers forcibly to remove Bowne's hat.

WHILE it gave no indication that it approved Stuyvesant's action in banishing Bowne, the committee seemed reluctant to interfere in a decision made by the provincial authorities in a matter involving violation of a local law. Instead, it was suggested that Bowne bring his wife and children to Holland to live since, the committee maintained, the company could not promise him liberty in New Netherland. Bowne replied that he had no intention of giving up his home in Flushing and that "liberty was promised to us in a patent given by virtue of the prince, the States General and the West India Company."

The committee observed that the patent had been granted by Governor Kieft "before any or but a few of your judgment (Quakers) were heard of."

"We are known to be a peaceful people," Bowne declared.

"But," the committee said, "if you will not be subject to the laws and placards which are published we cannot suffer you in our jurisdiction."

"It is good to consider whether the law or placard that was published be according to justice and righteousness, or whether it be not contrary to it, and also to that liberty promised us in our patent," Bowne argued.

Bowne had had the forethought to bring a copy of the Flushing patent with him, and urged the committee to read it. After due consideration of the document, the committee admitted that it found the patent "very good and like it well."

Finally it was decided that if Bowne would sign a bill of particulars the committee would recommend that he be allowed to return home. Bowne was admonished, however, that "all those that will not be subject to that placard (the ordinance against harboring Quakers) and all others (laws) that either are already there or shall hereafter be made, shall not live in our jurisdiction." Bowne refused to sign the document the committee prepared. Instead he presented the following written appeal:

"The paper drawn for me to sign I have perused and weighed, and do find the same not according to that engagement to me through one of your members, that he or you would do therein by me as you would be done unto, and not otherwise. For which of you being taken from your wife and family without just cause, would be found from returning to them unless upon terms to act contrary to your conscience, and deny your faith and religion, and yet in this effect do you require of me but not less.

"But truly, I cannot think that you did in sober earnest ever think I would subscribe to any such thing, it being the very thing for which I rather chose freely to suffer want of the company of my dear wife and children, imprisonment of my person, the ruin of my estate in my absence, and the loss of my goods here, than to yield or consent to such unreasonable thing as you thereby would enjoy unto me.

"For which I am persuaded you will not only be judged in the sight of God, but by good and godly men, rather to have mocked at the oppression of the oppressed and added affliction to the afflicted than therein to have done unto me as you in the like case would be done unto you, which the royal cause of our God requires.

"I have with patience and moderation waited several weeks expecting justice from you, but behold, an addition to my oppression is the measure I receive.

"Wherefore I have this now to request for you, that the Lord will not lay this to your charge, but to give eyes to see, and hearts to do justice, that you may find mercy with the Lord in the day of judgment."

To this argument the committee could find but one answer. John Bowne was released the next day and permitted to return home.

THE trial and acquittal of John Bowne was the culmination of a struggle that had gone on for nearly fifteen years. By his obstinacy and courage, his refusal to compromise in his religious beliefs, John Bowne won more than his personal freedom. It must be remembered that he had been arrested, imprisoned and banished for violation of the very same ordinance that the people of Flushing had denounced in the Remonstrance. And the arguments John Bowne used in his defense closely followed the theme of the Remonstrance.

The disposition of his case brought an end to religious persecution in the colony and vindicated the people of Flushing who had taken a firm and valiant stand against interference with the inviolate right of every man to worship God according to the dictates of his own conscience and to be tolerant toward his fellow men.

The religious freedom won from the Dutch government was continued under the English administration which began in 1664. Governor Nichols, who led the expedition which captured New Netherland from the Dutch, confirmed the Flushing town patent with its provision for liberty of conscience. A few years later religious freedom became the law for the entire colony. At the first meeting at Hempstead in October, 1683, the Representative Assembly, with representatives from Flushing, Jamaica, Newtown and Hempstead attending, drafted the Charter of Liberties. This charter, the basic law of the colony until the Constitution of the United States was adopted with its Bill of Rights, included as one of its provisions a guarantee to the people against any form of religious persecution.

Thus, in a chain of events extending over many years, the high ideal of religious tolerance, proclaimed in the Remonstrance and put into practice in John Bowne's home, found acceptance as a fundamental principle of the freedom which is the heritage of all Americans. It has been the aim of the Bowne House Historical Society to capture some of the feeling and charm of this house when it was lived in by early generations of the Bowne family, and to place emphasis upon what Bowne House symbolizes, rather than upon its architecture* or upon museum perfection in the display of its contents.

---

* In the June, 1952 issue of the Journal of The American Institute of Architects, an article entitled: "New York's Architectural Heritage", listed The Bowne House as one of twenty "structures of *national* importance which should be preserved at all costs."

"The spirit of liberty is the spirit which is not too sure that it is right; the spirit of liberty is the spirit which seeks to understand the minds of other men and women; the spirit of liberty is the spirit which weighs their interests alongside its own without bias; the spirit of liberty remembers that not even a sparrow falls to earth unheeded; the spirit of liberty is the spirit of Him who, near two thousand years ago, taught mankind that lesson it has never learned, but has never quite forgotten; that there may be a kingdom where the least shall be heard and considered side by side with the greatest."—Learned Hand

The Flushing
Issued on

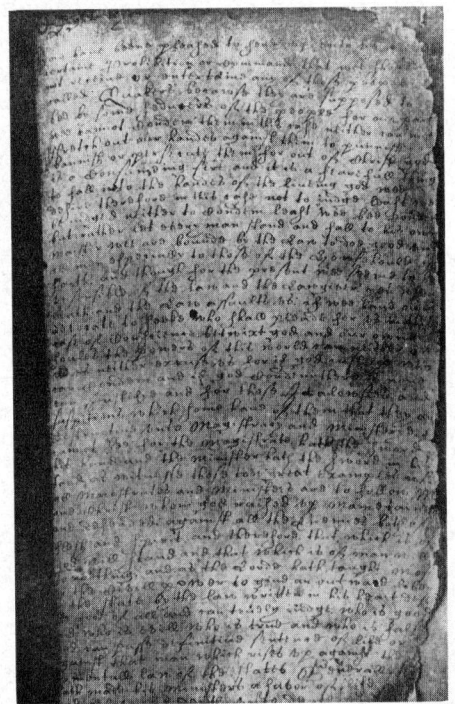
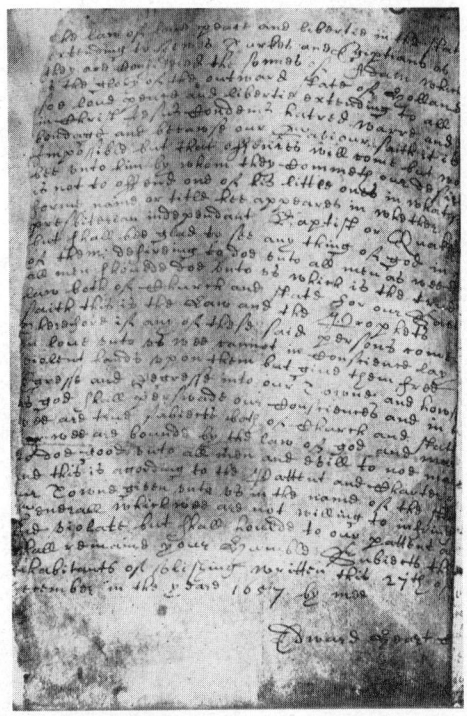
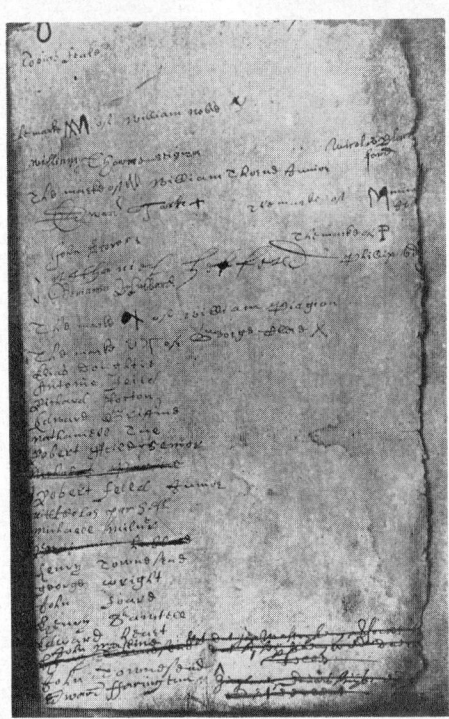

Facsimile of Original Manuscript
Manuscripts and History Section of the New York State Library in Albany

Remonstrance

December 27, 1657

Right Honorable,

You have been pleased to send up unto us a certain prohibition or command that we should not receive or entertain any of those people called Quakers because they are supposed to be by some, seducers of the people. For our part we cannot condemn them in this case, neither can we stretch out our hands against them, to punish, banish or persecute them, for out of Christ God is a consuming fire, and it is a fearful thing to fall into the hands of the living God.

Wee desire therefore in this case not to judge least we be judged, neither to condemn least we be condemned, but rather let every man stand and fall to his own Master. Wee are bounde by the Law to doe good unto all men, especially to those of the household of faith. And though for the present we seem to be unsensible of the law and the Law giver, yet when death and the Law assault us, if wee have our advocate to seeke, who shall plead for us in this case of conscience betwixt God and our own souls; the powers of this world can neither attack us, neither excuse us, for if God justifye who can condemn and if God condemn there is none can justifye.

And for those jealousies and suspicions which some have of them, that they are destructive unto Magistracy and Ministerye, that can not bee, for the magistrate hath the sword in his hand and the minister hath the sword in his hand, as witnesse those two great examples which all magistrates and ministers are to follow, Moses and Christ, whom God raised up maintained and defended against all the enemies both of flesh and spirit; and therefore that which is of God will stand, and that which is of man will come to nothing. And as the Lord hath taught Moses or the civil power to give an outward liberty in the state by the law written in his heart designed for the good of all, and can truly judge who is good, who is evil, who is true and who is false, and can pass definitive sentence of life or death against that man which rises up against the fundamental law of the States General; soe he hath made his ministers a savor of life unto life, and a savor of death unto death.

The law of love, peace and liberty in the states extending to Jews, Turks, and Egyptians, as they are considered the sonnes of Adam, which is the glory of the outward state of Holland, soe love, peace and liberty, extending to all in Christ Jesus, condemns hatred, war and bondage. And because our Saviour saith it is impossible but that offenses will come, but woe unto him by whom they cometh, our desire is not to offend one of his little ones, in whatsoever form, name or title hee appears in, whether Presbyterian, Independent, Baptist or Quaker, but shall be glad to see anything of God in any of them, desiring to doe unto all men as wee desire all men should doe unto us, which is the true law both of Church and State; for our Saviour saith this is the law and the prophets.

Therefore if any of these said persons come in love unto us, we cannot in conscience lay violent hands upon them, but give them free egresse and regresse unto our Town, and houses, as God shall persuade our consciences. And in this we are true subjects both of Church and State, for we are bounde by the law of God and man to doe good unto all men and evil to noe man. And this is according to the patent and charter of our Towne, given unto us in the name of the States General, which we are not willing to infringe, and violate, but shall houlde to our patent and shall remaine, your humble subjects, the inhabitants of Vlishing.

Written this 27th of December, in the year 1657, by me

EDWARD HEART, *Clericus*

Tobias Feake

The Marke of
William Noble

William Thorne, seignior

The Marke of
William Thorne, junior

Edward Tarne

John Store

Nathaniel Hefferd

Benjamin Hubbard

The Marke of
William Pidgion

The Marke of
George Clere

Elias Doughtie

Antonie Feild

Richard Stocton

Edward Griffine

Nathaniell Tue

Nicolas Blackford

The Marke of
Micah Tue

The Marke of
Philipp Ud

Robert Field, senior

Robert Field, junior

Nick Colas Parsell

Michael Milner

Henry Townsend

George Wright

John Foard

Henry Semtell

Edward Heart

John Mastine

John Townesend

Edward Farrington

Interior and Furnishings of Bowne House

IT WAS in the kitchen that the first meetings of Quakers were held, in defiance of Governor Stuyvesant's ban on the sect, resulting in Bowne's arrest and banishment from the New Netherland colony.

The dining room was added in 1680 and in 1696, a year after Bowne's death, his son, Samuel, built the living room, with the present entry, and more bedrooms on the upper floor. This section had the New England salt box style of architecture, with the roof on the back, or Fox Lane side, sloping to the ground. The only other change made in the house was in 1830, when the old roof was elevated and the north wing added, consisting of the guest room and library, and additional chambers.

THE KITCHEN, the oldest part of the house, has been arranged to give some of the atmosphere of the time when John and Hannah Bowne occupied it. In early colonial times, the kitchen was the center of all family activity. Besides cooking and eating, it was used for washing, spinning, weaving, preserving food, storing a variety of household articles and as a general living room. When the family overflowed the bedrooms upstairs, or an occasional visitor remained overnight, the kitchen also served as sleeping quarters.

JOHN BOWNE built the fireplace large enough to roast an ox if he had a mind to. The fire was never allowed to go out, being "raked up" with ashes when cooking was done. The bee-hive type oven, in the back of the fireplace, originally was exposed to the outdoors but in recent years was covered with a lean-to.

DUTCH HALF-DOORS, with the old iron stirrup knocker and latch, open into a small hall at the entrance to Bowne House. The narrow stairway, going up from the rear of the entry, is unusually perfect in its treads and only slightly worn despite long years of use. A small closet under the stairway is typical of the way in which every bit of space in the house is utilized.

THE INTERIOR walls of the living room are noteworthy for the unusually fine old wood panelling. The display of miniature furniture, dating from 1800, in the corner closet of this room, consists of what probably were samples of the wares of itinerant cabinet-makers, purchased as toys for the children. Another interesting exhibit is the cane with which Thomas Bowne, John's father, killed a bear. Lacking a weapon when the animal attacked him as he strolled down the lane from the house to what is now Northern Boulevard, Thomas Bowne had the presence of mind to thrust his cane down the bear's throat. The low, narrow doorway leading into the library is similar to those throughout the interior of the house.

Interior and Furnishings
(Continued)

THE HIGHBOY in the dining room is a very fine example of the William and Mary style, with trumpet legs, and the chairs around the table are of the early Queen Anne period. A tall eight-day clock, believed to have been made in Manhattan by Anthony Ward about 1735, has been keeping time all these many years. Hung in this room are portraits of Samuel Bowne (1812-90) and his wife, Elizabeth Ackerly Bowne (1814-75), painted by Francois Anelli in 1835 and loaned by the Museum of the City of New York.

IN THE RESTORATION program for Bowne House, wainscoting added in comparatively recent years was removed from the dining room, revealing the original hand-hewn beams put in place when the room was built in 1680. A glassed panel has been placed in what once was the back wall of the house, to show the use of straw and clay between horizontal oak supports—called "cobbing"—in its construction. The fireplace has the original hand-made brick and fire backs. Over it, built into the wall, are two long drawers in which were kept flint and rush tapers for lighting the fire, candles, herbs and pipes.

WHEN THE CLOCK STRIKES
I   Joy!
II Fear not.
III God is love.
IV In everything give thanks.
V   My peace I leave you.
VI Let not your heart be troubled.
VII May God supply you all you need!
VIII Fear thou not for I am with thee.
IX The Lord is my shepherd, I shall not want.
X   They that wait upon the Lord shall renew their strength.
XI Blessed be the pure in heart for they shall see God.
XII Bless the Lord, O my soul, and forget thou not His benefits.

THE MASSIVE mahogany secretary, beautifully hand-carved and with the original brass hardware, is believed to have been made in Manhattan between 1735 and 1750 especially for the living room.

SINCE 1735 this clock has chimed out the hours, marking the passing of time as perfectly today as when it was first made! Tacked inside the clock case is the reminder, "When the clock strikes," printed on brittle yellowed paper, date and author unknown.

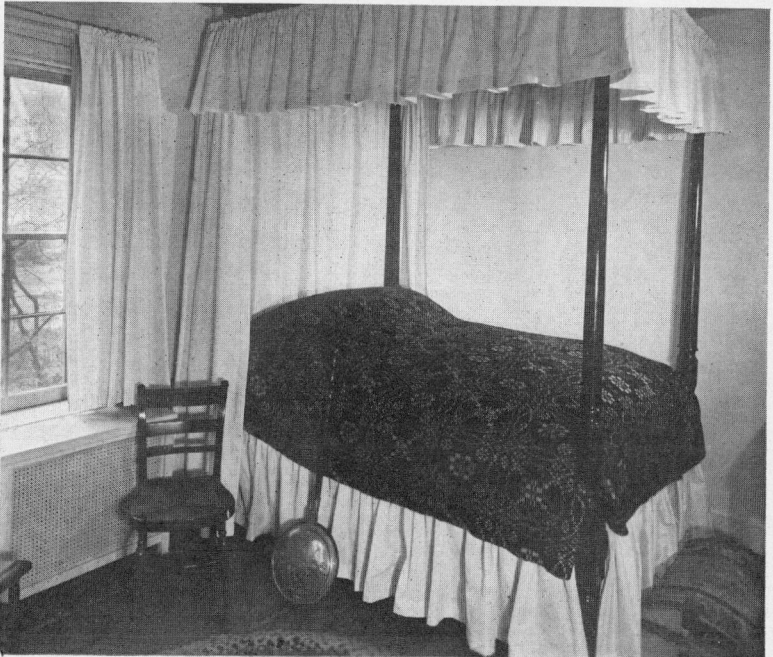

A SHERATON style four-poster feather bed is in the small guest room at the front of the house. Some of the family samplers hang on the walls. The bed warmer, used from early colonial times, was an essential piece of furniture in unheated rooms. The metal pan, attached to a long handle, was filled with hot coals and rubbed between the sheets before retiring on a cold night.

The Bowne House Historical Society

Margaret I. Carman[*]

THE name of an organization, like the name of an individual, may connote much or it may connote little; it may recall the traditions of a nation or be as impersonal as John Doe. Not until it has satisfied certain standards can it properly be considered an entity. One may ask, then: What is The Bowne House Historical Society? Why has it been organized? What has it accomplished? When these questions have been answered, the name of The Bowne House Historical Society will evoke a warm glow of pride in its heritage and a desire to further its mission.

No more adequate answers to the first two questions could be given than those found in the Provisional Charter which states that the Society "shall be a non-stock Corporation organized and operated exclusively for educational purposes."

The Society, having acquired ownership of Bowne House, is, under the Charter, required

> "To hold, maintain and preserve the same as an historical edifice of national interest intimately associated with events of profound significance in the establishment in this country of the fundamental principles of freedom of conscience and religious liberty; to encourage and maintain interest in the early history of the town of Flushing and to inaugurate and encourage historical research relative to the Bowne House and the events that transpired therein; to collect and preserve books, manuscripts, papers, relics and antiques relating to the early history of the town of Flushing; to mark or otherwise designate places of historical interest in said town or in territory adjacent thereto; to initiate and foster meetings and observances in commemoration of the historical events which have taken place in the Bowne House or in the town of Flushing, and to cultivate interest in such matters among school children."

The third question can best be answered by the achievements of the Society during the seven years of its existence.

JULY 27, 1945, and October 10, 1950, mark the five year probationary period during which the Society experienced the usual trials and tribulations of the probationer. However, there were many compensating moments of pleasure in real accomplishment for those whose efforts made the dream of the Bowne House, as a Shrine to Religious Liberty, a reality.

With the three hundredth anniversary of the founding of Flushing on October 10, 1645, fast approaching, a communication was read at a meeting of the Flushing Chamber of Commerce, held on February 15, 1945, from Mr. John J. Halleran, the President of the Flushing Historical Society, requesting cooperation in the planning of a tercentenary celebration. A week later Supreme Court Justice Charles S. Colden accepted Mr. Halleran's invitation to act as the General Chairman. Then followed a period of earnest, careful planning which later bore rich fruit.

To give purpose and direction to the celebration, the purchase, by public subscription, of the home of John Bowne, became the chief tangible goal of the tercentenary. Under the enthusiastic leadership of Judge Colden, an option to purchase the house for $35,000 was signed on May 7, 1945, and a week later the citizens of Flushing, meeting in the old Town Hall, approved the project. From that date on, the activities of the two groups, the Flushing Tercentenary Celebration Committee and the projected Bowne House Historical Society, paralleled and complemented each other until the conclusion of the celebration in October, 1945.

Nowhere was the significance of Bowne House more eloquently stated than by the New York Sun, when it observed editorially on October 6, 1945:

> "In choosing a theme for celebration of its tercentenary, the people of Flushing, Long

---

[*] The author of this article is a member of the Board of Trustees of The Bowne House Historical Society and its Historian. She is a member of the faculty of the Flushing High School.

MAYOR Fiorello H. LaGuardia with three direct descendants of John and Hannah Bowne—Miss Anna H. Parsons, Miss Bertha R. Parsons and Mr. William Bowne Parsons.

Island, wisely decided to pay high tribute to the memory of John Bowne. On next Wednesday Bowne House will be formally dedicated as a national shrine of religious tolerance. There in the 1660's Quakers met despite the ban imposed on their assembly for worship. British-born John Bowne, who had come to Flushing from Boston, was imprisoned by authorities in New Amsterdam and banished. But he was not to be driven from his belief, whatever the course of his exile.

"In Amsterdam, Holland, he was tried, and finally permitted to return vindicated to Long Island. The Quaker record as quoted by the Dictionary of American Biography provides a perfect memorial: 'He did Freely Expose him selfe his house and Esteate to ye service of Truth And had a Constant Meeting in his house neare About forty years. He Also suffered very much for ye truths seak.' Bowne House now becomes an inspiring shrine that may symbolize Milton's line, 'Hard are the ways of truth and rough to walk.'"

WHILE Flushing was buzzing with preparation for the tercentenary celebration during the week of October 7, 1945, Judge Colden, as the General Chairman, made the most of the current enthusiasm to set the infant Society on its feet. On August 2, 1945 its incorporators held their first meeting. Present were Judge Colden, Harry L. Dayton, John J. Halleran, Douglas G. Hardgrove, Samuel D. Jones, William Bowne Parsons, Le Roy T. Stratton, Mrs. Edward J. Streator and Haynes Trébor. Much was accomplished at this meeting; the by-laws were adopted, the incorporators were designated as the first trustees of the Society and temporary officers were elected. Mr. John J. Halleran expressed his desire to present to the Society a corporate seal. Needless to say, his gift was gratefully accepted.

Having set up the machinery for the operation of the Society, the first annual meeting of the membership was called. These were the persons who

MAYOR Fiorello H. LaGuardia broadcasting from the living room of Bowne House on October 7, 1945.

PRESIDENT Colden and Mayor LaGuardia after the broadcast.

up to then had subscribed to the purchase of the Bowne House. Immediately following this meeting, the trustees met and designated the following persons to serve as the first permanent officers:

CHARLES S. COLDEN, *President*
LE ROY T. STRATTON, *Vice-President*
SHERMAN S. ELY, *Treasurer*
MRS. EDWARD J. STREATOR, *Secretary*

One of the first acts of the trustees was to elect, as the first Life Members of the Society, Miss Bertha R. Parsons, Miss Anna H. Parsons, Mrs. William Bowne Parsons and William Bowne Parsons. This was as it should be because when formal delivery of the title to Bowne House was finally made, it came from "Anna H. Parsons and William B. Parsons, surviving executors for Mary B. Parsons." Mr. Parsons and his two sisters were direct descendants of John Bowne, in whose family ownership of the house had remained since it was built in 1661.

The fast-growing Society now concentrated its efforts on the events of the tercentenary celebration. Through the enthusiastic cooperation of the press, the eyes of the nation turned to Flushing in grateful appreciation of the part it had played in the age-old struggle for freedom. Broadcasting from the living room of Bowne House on October 7, 1945, Fiorello H. LaGuardia, the Mayor of the City of New York, said:

"This is a shrine; it belongs to our city, because it made so much history here, of endurance and fortitude. It belongs to our country because it is typical of America, and it belongs to the world because it is a symbol of what the world is looking for today."

ON the 10th of October, 1945, Mayor LaGuardia's words became officially a fact when, in the presence of thousands of people, the Bowne House was dedicated as "A National Shrine to Religious Freedom and Tolerance." Judge Colden presided at the dedication. To him was given the gratification of seeing realized that which many had thought could never be accomplished.

Seated on the grandstand in front of Bowne House that afternoon were dignitaries representing the national, state, city and borough governments,

PRESIDENT Colden making his address of welcome at the dedication of Bowne House on October 10, 1945, as a National Shrine to Religious Freedom.

The Netherlands Embassy and various religious faiths. Among those present were: United States Senator James M. Mead; Queens Borough President James A. Burke; Honorable George U. Harvey; Honorable Bernard M. Patten; Colonel James A. Roe; Brigadier General George J. Lawrence; Dr. Jacobus G. deBeus, Counselor of The Netherlands Embassy; Dr. Edward H. Brinton and Dr. Albert B. Corey. The clergy were represented by Dr. Charles H. Campbell, Reformed Dutch Church; Rev. B. A. Galloway, Macedonia A. M. E. Church; Dr. Norman A. Hall, First Methodist Church; Rev. Dougald L. MacLean, St. George's Episcopal Church; Rabbi Max Meyer, Free Synagogue; Monsignor John D. Wynne, St. Michael's Roman Catholic Church; Rev. E. Wallace Mast, Congregational Church, all of Flushing, and Rev. Archie Buchanan, Grace Episcopal Church of Whitestone.

DISTINGUISHED guests at the Dedicatory Exercises *l.* to *r.* Bernard M. Patten, George U. Harvey, James A. Burke, former Presidents of the Borough of Queens; Judge Colden; Senator James A. Mead and Colonel James A. Roe.

Senator James M. Mead made the address of dedication emphasizing that there must be "a militant John Bowne in each generation to be ever watchful that the written words of the charters be held sacred." Dr. Edward H. Brinton, the Director of the School for the Study of Social and Religious Sciences of Pendle Hill, Pa., representing the Quakers, recalled the career of Hannah Bowne, John Bowne's wife, mother of eight children, who, feeling called upon to do the Lord's work, went abroad to preach the Quaker faith in England, Ireland, and Germany.

One of the most human touches of the dedication was the presentation of a scroll to Dr. Jacobus G. deBeus, Counselor of The Netherlands Embassy, from the Town of Flushing, New York, to the Town of Flushing (Vlissengen), Holland. This presentation was symbolic of the interest and sympathy of the people of Flushing in the new world for the inhabitants of Flushing in the old, who, during the Second World War, had suffered much from bombing and floods when their dikes were destroyed.

DISTINGUISHED guests at the Dedicatory Exercises *l.* to *r.* Monsignor John D. Wynne, Pastor of St. Michael's Roman Catholic Church; Dr. Albert B. Corey, New York State Historian; Reverend B. A. Galloway, Macedonia A. M. E. Church; Reverend E. Wallace Mast, Pastor of the Congregational Church.

The tercentenary celebration successfully concluded, and the Bowne House acquired free and clear of indebtedness, two gigantic tasks confronted the Society: preparation of the house and grounds for early opening to the public, and the active functioning of the Society in as large a sphere as possible.

Many, many hands and hearts set to work to attain these important objectives. To list the names of those responsible for accomplishing these Gargantuan tasks in so short a time, would be well nigh impossible. Like the ever-widening circles from a pebble cast into a pond, the full extent of their influence will never be known. Of necessity, a heavier load was borne by some than by others. None was heavier than that of President Colden. His vision, his faith, his wisdom and his tireless patient devotion to the preservation of this symbol of the true meaning of America, inspired all who worked with him.

DR. JACOBUS G. de BEUS, Counselor of The Netherlands Embassy, addressing the audience at the dedication of Bowne House.

FIRST'S are always interesting. The first time the trustees conducted their meeting in Bowne House was on June 24, 1946. The number in attendance on that memorable occasion was more than twice that of the first meeting in 1945. Present were:

    CHARLES S. COLDEN, *presiding*
    DR. CHARLES H. CAMPBELL
    HARRY L. DAYTON
    MRS. PAUL B. FINDLEY
    W. FLEMER FOULK
    ARTHUR H. GREELEY
    MRS. LAURENCE B. HALLERAN
    DOUGLAS G. HARDGROVE
    SAMUEL D. JONES
    RABBI MAX MEYER
    MISS ANNA M. O'CONNOR
    HAROLD G. PARKER
    WILLIAM BOWNE PARSONS
    CHARLES U. POWELL
    FRANKLIN F. REGAN
    LE ROY T. STRATTON
    MRS. EDWARD J. STREATOR
    HAYNES TRÉBOR
    WILLIAM H. WAECHTER

The first step towards the renovation of Bowne House was taken at this time. On motion of Samuel D. Jones, the House Committee was authorized "to proceed to do as much in the way of restoration of the Bowne House as is possible for the sum of $2,000." Plans for restoration of the house materialized very rapidly and a House Committee was appointed consisting of Mr. Laurence B. Halleran, chairman, Mrs. Laurence B. Halleran, Samuel D. Jones, Mrs. John H. Tennent, Miss Mary MacLeod, Miss Anna M. O'Connor, and Le Roy T. Stratton.

Mrs. Halleran consulted Mr. Joseph Downs, Curator of the American Wing of the Metropolitan Museum of Art, who advised restoration of part rather than of the whole house at this time. Consequently, restoration was confined to the first floor of the building.

To preserve as authentic an atmosphere as possible, Mr. Laurence B. Halleran was authorized to purchase from Mr. William Bowne Parsons, for the sum of $1,000, certain articles already in the Bowne House. Mr. Parsons donated other articles, valuable chiefly in that they added to the general charm of the house. A short time later, a very beautiful desk and pewter teacups and bowls, which had formerly been in the house, were acquired—the first of many interesting acquisitions—now a part of its furnishings.

JUST as most American families observe some occasions peculiarly significant to them, so the Bowne House Historical Society has developed the tradition of having three annual celebrations: Independence Day on July 4; Founders' Day on October 10, marking the granting of the charter on that day in 1645 to found the Town of Flushing; and Remonstrance Day on December 27, in honor of the inhabitants of Flushing who on December 27, 1657, sent a remonstrance to Governor Stuyvesant protesting his ban against the Quakers.

The first celebration of Independence Day by the Society was in 1947 and coincided with the official opening of Bowne House to the public. When the house was purchased, it was the home of the Misses Anna and Bertha Parsons. In deference to their wishes the Society had held most of its meetings elsewhere and did not formally open the house to the public until such time as the Parsons family no longer wished to occupy it. Not until April 1, 1947, did the Society take actual physical possession of its property.

From then until Opening Day, the house was in the throes of excitement and activity. The grounds were made neat and trim. On the front lawn, Mr. William J. Halleran had erected, without cost to the Society, an appropriate new flagpole on which would be flown a new flag, the gift of Mr. William Bowne Parsons. The Flushing Historical Society presented a beautifully engrossed Guest Book in which Miss Edna L. Franklin, a direct descendant of John and Hannah Bowne, was the first to register.

Perhaps the most important part of the preparation for Opening Day, and indeed thereafter, was the formation of a staff of volunteer hostesses who would conduct visitors through the house. Mrs. Laurence B. Halleran, chairman of the Hostesses Committee, had no difficulty whatever in finding thirty women to assist in this vital phase of the work of the Society. Upon this group of volunteers devolved the responsibility for establishing the Bowne House Story in the minds of visitors who, in turn, might promote further interest in the Society and its work. Judge Colden's tribute to this Committee emphasized its importance: "Those who come to the Bowne House are learning of its significance, many for the first time. This has never been so important as it is today. Bowne House stands for something so very real in the face of world-wide conditions that it is truly a shrine of national importance. This group of enthusiastic and devoted women give unselfishly of their time to tell the story over and over again to people who come here from all parts of our country and from overseas. Those who hear the story learn the real meaning of religious freedom born as a result of personal suffering and hardship."

On the morning of July 4, 1947, Bowne House was officially opened to the public, and the annual celebration of Independence Day became a part of the Society's program. Between four hundred and five hundred persons attended the exercises and visited the house during the day. The President of the Society delivered an inspiring address, stressing the significance of the occasion and expressing the hope that at this historic spot, on succeeding Independence Days, citizens would assemble to honor the memory of those who had sacrificed so much for the freedom we now enjoy. The sentiments of those who had been privileged to attend the opening exercises found expression in a sonnet which Judge Colden received a few days later:

"*Little House on Bowne Street*
The gentle magic of the twilight hour,
Drifts down the soft, sweet evening air where waits
Not merely one small cot with tree and flower;
But truly—all of these United States.
Ten thousand years ago, the glaciers came;
The timeless waters still break on these banks;
Here spread religious freedom like a flame;
Here men and women offered tearful thanks.
Now, where the stars eternal, gravely nod
And men around the earth, in sorrow stand,
Our hearts turn to this covenant with God,
And bless the fate that made us of this land.
Where rose-flush curtains of young dawn will roll
On this clapboard cathedral of the soul."

—*Ed McNamee*

The first celebration of Founders' Day coincided with the dedication on October 10, 1945, of the Bowne House as a National Shrine to Religious Freedom. Memorable observances of that day followed annually and included such events as the dedication of the John Bowne School and the presentation by Dr. Albert B. Corey, Director, Division of Archives and History of the New York State Department of Education, of the Society's Absolute Charter, bringing to a successful close its first five-year period of existence.

The first celebration of Remonstrance Day, planned for December 27, 1947, was particularly significant because for two hundred and ninety years there had not been a public observance of that day. The first attempt to celebrate the occasion had to be postponed to January 24, 1948, because of a blizzard. Another severe snowstorm almost cancelled the postponed exercises. However, about seventy-five persons braved the storm and attended the exercises in the Quaker Meeting House on Northern Boulevard, Flushing. Then they tramped through the snowstorm to Bowne House, where a delightful reception by candlelight was awaiting them. Dr. Charles S. Gosnell, New York State Librarian, made a special trip from Albany to exhibit the original Remonstrance, which is preserved in the State Library. Over the hearth in the kitchen of Bowne House, where John Bowne first permitted Quakers to conduct religious services in defiance of Governor Peter Stuyvesant's ban in 1662, there was placed on this occasion a beautifully engrossed legend composed by Judge Colden, reading as follows:

"IN THIS ROOM
AN OPPRESSED PEOPLE
FOUND SANCTUARY

Here lived John Bowne Who Suffered Arrest, Imprisonment, Separation from His Home, His Wife And Children, and Banishment to the Old World, So That a Then Despised People Might Worship God in This Room and In the New World in The Manner of Their Own Choosing. HERE WAS BORN RELIGIOUS FREEDOM IN THE AMERICAN WAY OF LIFE."

IN TIME, the varied activities of the Bowne House Historical Society became better known and many individuals and groups began to give it recognition.

The Flushing Council of Women's Organizations donated $100 "to initiate an endowment fund for the maintenance of Bowne House and for carrying out the purposes of the Society." Later, when the National Freedom Train visited Flushing in December, 1948, the President of the Society, Judge Colden, and a representative group of members were invited to participate. At the dedication exercises held in the Quaker Meeting House on Northern Boulevard, Flushing, on December 10, 1948, Judge Colden delivered the principal address. The assemblage then renewed the Freedom Pledge which significantly embodies the principles for which John Bowne sacrificed so much.

"THE FREEDOM PLEDGE
I am an American, a free American
Free to speak—without fear
Free to worship God in my own way,
Free to stand for what I think right,
Free to oppose what I believe wrong,
Free to choose those who govern my country.
This heritage of freedom I pledge to uphold
For myself and all mankind."

At first, Bowne House was opened to visitors on Tuesdays and Saturdays from three to five in the afternoon. As the number of visitors increased, it was considered expedient to include Sunday afternoons also, since many persons could not conveniently attend on the other visiting days.

On the introductory page of the Visitors' Register is the following quotation: "The ornaments of a house are the friends that frequent it." Bowne House, then, should be especially adorned because, to date, approximately 25,000 persons have visited it, many from distant states and from every continent.

One visitor, from England, noted on the Register: "This is my first historical visit in America. The house is fascinating; full of precious ghosts." Another, was a little boy, only six years of age, accompanied by his mother who guided his hand as he signed the Register, "John Bowne." The little boy was a John Bowne of the tenth generation. Sometime later a displaced teen-age German boy was observed listening with rapt attention to every word of the hostess as she described the significance of the building. He first heard of the Bowne House when he was a prisoner in Germany and had then vowed to make a pilgrimage if he ever regained his freedom and came to America.

These incidents are just a few since Bowne House was opened seven years ago as a shrine to religious freedom in America, but they are illustrative of the important work accomplished by the staff of hostesses under the leadership of Mrs. Laurence B.

Halleran, who deserves special recognition. Day after day during these seven years she has conducted and arranged with other hostesses on her staff to guide groups of school children through the House. With charm of manner and patient understanding, the seeds of true Americanism have thus been sown among thousands of those who will be the citizens of tomorrow.

While the rapidity with which Bowne House was being accepted by the public gratified the members of the Society, it worried the House Committee for it meant more visitors. The 1946 appropriation of $2,000 for restoration had been exhausted before the house had been opened to the public. From sources never dreamed of, financial contributions were made from time to time. These varied in amount, but large or small, they all stressed the fine quality of the work which the Society is doing.

PARTICULARLY notable among those who contributed to the development of the Society's program was Queens Borough Lodge of the Benevolent and Protective Order of Elks, which, through the interest of a good friend and member, Supreme Court Justice James T. Hallinan, has each year included the Society in its annual distribution of gifts to hospitals, charitable, welfare, civic and patriotic agencies. The Flushing Savings Bank did much to further the work and fame of the Society. Its officers and trustees adopted a program of advertising which includes emphasis upon the rich heritage of the historic contributions of the old colonial town of Flushing. As part of this program, the bank has sponsored the printing of the various publications of the Society, including "The Flushing Remonstrance" and "Bowne House—A Shrine To Religious Freedom."

A most encouraging event took place on July 17, 1951, when the Trustees and the Committee of Hostesses of the Society were the guests of the New York Telephone Company in Flushing at the unveiling of a large and beautifully colored enlargement of a photograph of an old print entitled: "Mr. Bowne's House in America." The significance of this gracious act of civic cooperation cannot be overestimated since as many as 25,000 persons visiting the office monthly are thus reminded that in their community stands this historic Shrine to Religious Freedom.

The financial cooperation received from many well-wishers spurred the House Committee in its efforts to make more of the building available to the ever-increasing number of visitors. By April, 1950, the entire first floor, including the shed in the rear, had been restored; and shortly thereafter, two large front rooms on the second floor were made ready.

Interesting decorative touches were not overlooked. After extensive research by Miss Nancy McClelland, an authority on period decoration, the Scalamandré Studio of New York generously donated and hung throughout the house specially woven period curtains and draperies. These complemented the furnishings in the various rooms and created a charming and homelike atmosphere. In addition, every effort was made to improve the gardens and thus provide a more attractive setting for the historic old house. The Society was fortunate, indeed, in having two members, Mrs. Samuel D. Jones and Miss Mary N. Dixon, thoroughly qualified to plan and supervise this work. To identify and label correctly the trees and shrubs on the grounds, they received the cooperation of Mr. Everett Martin, Mrs. William Astle, and Mr. Roland Schultheis, each an expert in this field. The identification was verified by Dr. Clarence Lewis of the Farmingdale Horticultural and Agricultural School and the aluminum tape identification labels, made by students under his direction, were donated by Mr. and Mrs. Samuel D. Jones.

Nearly 3,000 bulbs have been planted in various parts of the grounds. Two lovely flowering almond trees bend their graceful pink sprays towards the sun dial; a rare silver bell-tree blossoms at one end of the soft, velvety lawn. To describe the variety of colors that come and go with the seasons is impossible—tulips, daffodils, violets, peonies, roses, Madonna lilies, petunias, and boxwood—all are there. Even in late January little blossoming snowdrops have been seen, snuggling up to the front of the house, which faces the south as did most of the colonial, "salt-box" houses. As the seasons change, two things remain the same: the clump of tall, bamboo grasses by the kitchen door, and the gracefulness of the lovely Japanese maple shading in lacey pattern the old settee on the quaint front porch.

EVEN with such a lovely garden and grounds as a setting, the Society was not completely satisfied. It is recorded in the secretary's minutes that Mayor La Guardia "broadcasting from the living room of the Bowne House on Sunday afternoon, October 7, 1945, disclosed plans for a new City Park with Bowne House as the focal center." Into the very capable hands of our treasurer, Mr. Franklin F. Regan, was entrusted the task of making Mayor La Guardia's statement come true. By January, 1947, a map of the proposed extension to Weeping Beech Park (Bowne Street and 37th Avenue, Flushing) was filed with the Board of Estimate by the Queens Commissioner of Public Works, along with a request that the property be acquired. In March, 1950, the Planning Commission reported favorably. Less than a year later, the Board of Estimate adopted a resolution vesting in the City of New York title to the property for Bowne House Park. Additional ground was added to the park area and it is only a matter of time before the setting of Bowne House will be enlarged by "a well-planned park on the east side of Bowne Street, running north from the Bowne property to the apartment building and running easterly so as to connect the present westerly line of 'Weeping Beech Park.'"

When this has been accomplished, one can again, standing on "Bowne" property, see two outstanding historic reminders. Across the road on Bowne Street a gray boulder marks the site of the Fox Oaks, twin trees under which George Fox, founder of the Society of Friends, preached in John Bowne's yard, in 1672. To the east, in majestic splendor, stands the largest and most beautiful weeping beech tree in the United States. In 1847 Samuel Bowne Parsons, a famous nurseryman, a descendant of John Bowne, planted the twig from which grew this tree, a cutting from "dwarfed" beech tree.

THERE is no way of adequately measuring and recording the amount of hard work that has made the Society the success it is today. In retrospect, however, certain tangible evidence bears witness. The John Bowne Story has been broadcast over two major networks—WOR and WCBS. A play, entitled "The Dawn's Early Light" based on the life of John Bowne, and written by John Golden, actor, director and producer and Haynes Trébor, a trustee of the Society, had a dramatic reading in the John Bowne School on October 24, 1950. A very fine Antiques Exhibit was held in the two upper front rooms of Bowne House on October 11, 12 and 13, 1950. The inspired work of Mrs. Laurence B. Halleran and Mrs. Paul B. Findley, co-chairmen, proved highly successful. Choice heirlooms of the Bowne Family and of other old Flushing families were so artistically arranged and displayed, that their beauty lingers in the memory of all who saw them.

Breathtaking, is it not, this even condensed story of the vigorous young Bowne House Historical Society. Five years ago Judge Colden spoke prophetic words when he said, "I feel that we are just at the beginning of something that will prove of value to our city, state and nation. Much has been accomplished, but much remains to be done. God willing, it shall be done!"

"It behooves every man who values liberty of conscience for himself, to resist invasions of it in the case of others—I never will, by any word or act, bow to the shrine of intolerance, or admit a right of inquiry into the religious opinions of others."—*Thomas Jefferson.*

An Appreciation

IT has been said that "He that would be the first among you, let him be your servant." I know of no one who better typifies the wisdom of this observation than the President of The Bowne House Historical Society—Charles S. Colden. An indefatigable worker in the service of his community, his career parallels the phenomenal growth of Queens from a suburban community to one which with its more than one and one-half million inhabitants is seventh in county population in the nation.

A direct descendant of Cadwallader Colden, Lieutenant Governor of New York Colony (1760-1775), and of Judge John Fell, Member of the Continental Congress, Judge Colden was born in Whitestone on the north shore of Queens County on June 3, 1885. He is a graduate of Whitestone Public School, Flushing High School and Jamaica State Normal School. A teacher in the public schools and principal of an evening school, he studied law and received his LL.B. and LL.M. degrees from the New York University School of Law in 1913. Admitted to the Bar the same year, he soon established himself as a leading lawyer and civic worker in the community in which he was born.

His public career began with his appointment as Assistant District Attorney of Queens County in 1918. He resumed the private practice of the law in 1922. Ten years later he was appointed District Attorney of Queens County by Governor Franklin D. Roosevelt and, in the fall of that year, was elected for a full term of three years. In 1935 he was appointed County Judge of Queens County by Governor Herbert H. Lehman and, in the fall of that year, was elected for a full term of fourteen years. In 1942 he was elected a Justice of the Supreme Court of the State of New York for a term of fourteen years, in which capacity he is now serving with distinction, and frequently is assigned for service in the Appellate Term of the Supreme Court, Second Judicial Department.

The father of many institutions in Queens, the crowning glory of his efforts is The Bowne House Historical Society and the establishment of Bowne House as a National Shrine to Religious Freedom. He conceived, organized and, since its inception, has been the President of the Queens College Association which brought about the establishment of Queens College in 1937. As President of the Queens County Bar Association in 1927-1928 he activated the movement which, due to his continued persistent efforts, resulted in the erection of that temple of justice in Jamaica, Long Island—the General Court House. In 1945 he was the Chairman of the Flushing Tercentenary Committee under whose auspices the people of Flushing celebrated the 300th anniversary of the granting of their charter.

Judge Colden has taken an active part in many other organizations in the county. He was one of the founders of and now is a trustee of the Flushing Savings Bank, having served also as its President and Chairman of the Board. He was President of the Queens College Speech and Hearing Center, which has done so much to aid children and adults suffering from speech and hearing defects. He is a director and past President of St. David's Society of the State of New York and a member of numerous other patriotic and historical societies. He is a director of the Society of the National Shrine of the Bill of Rights at St. Paul's Church, Eastchester, New York; Flushing Interfaith Society and of the Firemen's Home at Hudson, New York. He is the Senior Warden of Grace Episcopal Church, Whitestone, Long Island, and a lay member of the Chapter of the Cathedral of the Incarnation in Garden City, Long Island.

Limitations of space make it impossible further to enumerate the many other causes which Judge Colden has espoused in more than thirty-five years of public life. Teacher, lawyer, banker, jurist, citizen—in each capacity he gives unstintingly of his time and efforts, perceiving, guiding and supporting many worthwhile projects. He has earned the everlasting gratitude of his fellow citizens.—Editor.

Committees

OF

THE BOWNE HOUSE HISTORICAL SOCIETY

HOUSE
Laurence B. Halleran, *Chairman*

Mrs. Paul B. Findley	Douglas G. Hardgrove	Miss Anna M. O'Connor
Mrs. Laurence B. Halleran	Samuel D. Jones	LeRoy T. Stratton
William J. Halleran	Miss Mary MacLeod	Mrs. John H. Tennent

GENERAL PROGRAM AND EDUCATION
Rabbi Max Meyer, *Chairman*

Dr. Charles H. Campbell	Mrs. Edward J. Streator	Haynes Trébor
	William H. Waechter	

MEMBERSHIP
Douglas G. Hardgrove, *Chairman*

John J. Halleran	Miss Anna M. O'Connor	Haynes Trébor

PUBLICATIONS
Haynes Trébor, *Chairman*

Harry L. Dayton	Rabbi Max Meyer	William Bowne Parsons

TAX EXEMPTION
John J. Halleran, *Chairman*

Samuel D. Jones	Miss Anna M. O'Connor	Franklin F. Regan

ACQUISITIONS
Mrs. Paul B. Findley, *Chairman*

Laurence B. Halleran	Charles U. Powell

BOWNE HOUSE PARK
Franklin F. Regan, *Chairman*

Harry L. Dayton	Charles U. Powell

RESEARCH
Miss Margaret I. Carman, *Chairman*

Mrs. Paul B. Findley	Mrs. Edward J. Streator	Mrs. John H. Tennent

Committees (continued)

•

BY-LAWS

Franklin F. Regan, *Chairman*

Laurence B. Halleran   Miss Anna M. O'Connor

GARDEN

Mrs. Samuel D. Jones   Miss Mary N. Dixon

DESCENDANTS

Mrs. John H. Tennent, *Chairman*
Miss Emma S. Underhill
Mrs. Malcolm Sands Wilson

BOWNE HOUSE BOOK

Mrs. Edward J. Streator, *Chairman*

Miss Margaret I. Carman	Samuel S. Tripp, *Editor*	Franklin F. Regan
Laurence B. Halleran	Miss Anna M. O'Connor	Haynes Trébor

HOSTESSES

Mrs. Laurence B. Halleran, *Chairman*

Mrs. Hector Alexander	†Miss Edna L. Franklin	Mrs. Charles Reges
Miss Mary H. Averill	†Mrs. Richard Furman	Miss Matilda H. Roberts
Mrs. Clarence W. Brazer	*Mrs. H. Ellsworth Gelwicks	Mrs. Chester Rudolf
Miss Mary D. Bromham	†Mrs. Marion Bowne Gilbert	Mrs. Frederick C. Sasse
Miss Margaret I. Carman	†Mrs. Albert W. Humm	Mrs. Thomas G. Schaedle
*Mrs. Samuel A. Cox	Mrs. Samuel D. Jones	Mrs. Elmer W. Silver
Mrs. Walter T. Daub	Mrs. Louis Leggett	Mrs. Watson A. Silver
Mrs. Sheldon W. Dean	Miss Agnes Lyall	Mrs. Frederick S. Sly
Miss Helen S. Dixon	Mrs. Edward C. Moore	Mrs. Jean E. Smalbach
Miss Julia M. Fanning	Mrs. Alice Noble	†Mrs. John H. Tennent
Mrs. W. Philip Fickett	Miss Anna M. O'Connor	Mrs. Edwin Wheeler
Mrs. Paul B. Findley	Mrs. Duncan Parham	Mrs. H. C. Wightman
	Mrs. Alfred H. Rapp	

---

†Bowne Descendant
*Deceased

Membership

IN

THE BOWNE HOUSE HISTORICAL SOCIETY

•

The By-Laws of the Society provide that membership therein shall be divided into four classes: *Life, Patron, Sustaining and Regular.*

1. Life members of the Society shall be individuals who are elected thereto and who contribute to the Society, in lieu of annual dues, the sum of $250 or more.

2. Patron members of the Society shall be individuals who are elected thereto and pay the dues of either Regular or Sustaining members together with any additional sum that such Patron member may elect to contribute to the Society. In lieu of such additional sum, such Patron member may donate suitable articles of historic interest to the Society.

3. Sustaining members of the Society shall be individuals who pay annual dues of $10 on the day of enrollment and annually thereafter upon the 15th day of September in each year.

4. Regular members of the Society shall be individuals who pay annual dues of $5 on the day of enrollment and annually thereafter upon the 15th day of September in each year.

Life Members

OF

THE BOWNE HOUSE HISTORICAL SOCIETY

Max Abramson
Flushing, Long Island

Vincent Astor
New York City, New York

Bank of the Manhattan Company
Jamaica, Long Island

Bayside Federal Savings and Loan Association
Bayside, Long Island

†Mr. and Mrs. Edgar W. Bowne
Glen Head, Long Island

Burns Brothers
New York City, New York

Miss Margaret I. Carman
Flushing, Long Island

Claridge Food Company, Inc.
Flushing, Long Island

Honorable Charles S. Colden
Whitestone, Long Island

College Point Savings Bank
College Point, Long Island

Consolidated Edison Company of New York, Inc.
New York City, New York

Dr. Albert B. Corey, New York State Historian
Albany, New York

Corn Exchange Bank Trust Company
Flushing, Long Island

Miss Mary N. Dixon
Flushing, Long Island

Empire Mill Works Corporation
Corona, Long Island

Mrs. Paul B. Findley
Flushing, Long Island

*Honorable Maurice A. Fitzgerald
Kew Gardens, Long Island

William J. Fitzpatrick
Malba, Long Island

Flushing Cemetery Association
Flushing, Long Island

Flushing Chamber of Commerce
Flushing, Long Island

Flushing Merchants Association
Flushing, Long Island

Flushing Savings Bank
Flushing, Long Island

Flushing Storage Warehouse Company
Flushing, Long Island

W. Flemer Foulk
Flushing, Long Island

Walton S. Gagel
Maspeth, Long Island

†Bowne Descendant
*Deceased

*Mrs. H. Ellsworth Gelwicks
Flushing, Long Island

B. Gertz, Inc.
Jamaica, Long Island

Harry Gilbert
Flushing, Long Island

John Golden
Bayside, Long Island

Dr. Charles F. Gosnell, New York State Librarian
Albany, New York

Edward Gottlieb
Jamaica, Long Island

Honorable Thomas J. Gray
Jackson Heights, Long Island

Mrs. Laurence B. Halleran
Flushing, Long Island

John J. Halleran
Flushing, Long Island

Laurence B. Halleran
Flushing, Long Island

William J. Halleran
Flushing, Long Island

Honorable James T. Hallinan
Flushing, Long Island

Harry Heuman
Flushing, Long Island

*E. C. Hulst
Flushing, Long Island

Fenley Hunter
Flushing, Long Island

Gale Hunter
Essex, Connecticut

Samuel Day Jones
Flushing, Long Island

Thomas F. Kearns
Flushing, Long Island

Samuel Keepnews
Flushing, Long Island

Lily Tulip Cup Corporation
New York, New York

Joseph B. Linek
Elmhurst, Long Island

Lions Club of Flushing
Flushing, Long Island

Ernest S. Macdonald
New York, New York

MacGrotty Chevrolet Company, Inc.
Flushing, Long Island

Miss Nancy McClelland
New York, New York

George McGuire
Whitestone, Long Island

Merkel, Inc.
Jamaica, Long Island

Life Members (continued)

NATIONAL CITY BANK OF NEW YORK
New York, New York

*JOHN NEWBOLD
Whitestone, Long Island

COLONEL NORMAN N. NEWHOUSE
Jamaica, Long Island

THEODORE NEWHOUSE
Jamaica, Long Island

NEW YORK TELEPHONE COMPANY
New York City, New York

LAWRENCE G. NUSBAUM
Flushing, Long Island

*†MISS ANNA H. PARSONS
Flushing, Long Island

*†MISS BERTHA R. PARSONS
Flushing, Long Island

†REGINALD H. PARSONS
Medford, Oregon

†WILLIAM BOWNE PARSONS
Flushing, Long Island

*MRS. WILLIAM BOWNE PARSONS
Flushing, Long Island

JOHN H. POSSENREIDE
Winfield, Long Island

QUEENS BOROUGH LODGE OF ELKS NO. 878
Elmhurst, Long Island

QUEENS COUNTY SAVINGS BANK
Flushing, Long Island

†MRS. HENRY S. REDMOND
New York City, New York

---

†Bowne Descendant
*Deceased

FRANKLIN F. REGAN
Whitestone, Long Island

MR. AND †MRS. GILBERT W. ROBERTS
Manhasset, Long Island

CHARLES K. ROE
Flushing, Long Island

CLINTON T. ROE
New York City, New York

STEPHEN ROGERS
Long Island City, Long Island

FRANCO SCALAMANDRÉ
Long Island City, Long Island

HONORABLE MARTIN SCHWAEBER
Jamaica, Long Island

THE SOROPTIMIST CLUB OF NORTH SHORE QUEENS
Flushing, Long Island

LEROY T. STRATTON
Rutland, Vermont

MRS. EDWARD J. STREATOR
Bayside, Long Island

SYLVANIA ELECTRIC PRODUCTS, INC.
Bayside, Long Island

ARTHUR A. TEICHER
Flushing, Long Island

†MRS. JOHN H. TENNENT
Flushing, Long Island

HAYNES TRÉBOR
Flushing, Long Island

LOUIS O. TRILSCH
Whitestone, Long Island

WEBB AND KNAPP, INC.
New York City, New York

†MRS. EDITH KING WILSON
New York City, New York

Sustaining Members

OF

THE BOWNE HOUSE HISTORICAL SOCIETY

†Colonel Frederic Bowne
   Jackson Heights, New York

†Martin Starr Bowne
   Clearfield, Kentucky

†Thomas Martin Bowne
   New York City, New York

Benjamin Braunstein
   Flushing, Long Island

Miss Mary D. Bromham
   Whitestone, Long Island

†Francis Gordon Brown
   New York City, New York

Edmund G. Burke
   New York City, New York

William Canter
   Flushing, Long Island

Richard Carson
   Flushing, Long Island

Craig Colgate
   Flushing, Long Island

†Mrs. Ruth Bowne Connolly
   Las Charras, Venezuela

Thomas W. Constable
   New York City, New York

County Fuel Company, Inc.
   Flushing, Long Island

†Mrs. Rebecca L. Crouse
   Ithaca, New York

Dr. D. D. Daly
   New York City, New York

Exempt Fireman's Association of the Town of Newtown
   Elmhurst, Long Island

Free Synagogue of Flushing
   Flushing, Long Island

Honorable Edward R. Finch
   New York City, New York

First Congregational Church of Flushing
   Flushing, Long Island

Flushing Federal Savings and Loan Association
   Flushing, Long Island

†Bowne Descendant
*Deceased

†Mrs. Howard Frame
   Los Altos, California

Garden Club of Malba
   Malba, Long Island

A. Joseph Geist
   Belle Harbor, Long Island

John P. Gering
   Elmhurst, Long Island

Charles D. Gilbert
   Flushing, Long Island

Gladstone-Dasey Associates
   Flushing, Long Island

Wesley C. Hallett
   Flushing, Long Island

Peter C. Heidelberger
   Flemington, New Jersey

Mrs. Knut Hoegh Houck
   Flushing, Long Island

Dr. Knut Hoegh Houck
   Flushing, Long Island

†Mrs. Josiah Lasell, 2nd
   Litchfield, Connecticut

*†Townsend Lawrence
   New York City, New York

†Mrs. Zelia I. McCord
   Flushing, Long Island

†Mrs. John C. McPherson
   Short Hills, New Jersey

Rabbi Max Meyer
   Flushing, Long Island

Mr. and Mrs. George Miller
   Great Neck, Long Island

John V. O'Neill
   Jamaica Estates, Long Island

†Mrs. Arthur Pollion
   Princeton, New Jersey

Samuel J. Rosenthal
   Flushing, Long Island

John G. Steele
   Flushing, Long Island

James D. Stevens
   Flushing, Long Island

William H. Waechter
   Flushing, Long Island

Regular Members

OF

THE BOWNE HOUSE HISTORICAL SOCIETY

Ambrose B. Acker
Dr. Robert A. Adams
Honorable Frank F. Adel
Mr. and Mrs. Hector J. Alexander
American Association of University Women,
 Queens Branch
American Federation of Rubber Workers
 (Local #20499)
Anchor Lodge No. 729 F. and A. M.
†Mrs. Rupert Anderson
Mrs. Lucy Aring
Harold J. Ash
Miss Mary Halsey Averill
Dr. Herbert D. Ayers, Sr.

*Mrs. Philip Bach
Jesse R. Bacharach
Dr. and Mrs. Louis J. Bailey
Mrs. Kenneth H. Bailey
†Mrs. G. W. E. Baldwin
†Mrs. H. S. Bartow
Bayside National Bank of New York
Kendall Beaton
Mrs. Kendall Beaton
†Kenneth Beebe
Beechhurst Women's Club, Inc.
Frank A. Bellucci
Hugh G. Bergen
Alexander Berger
Mrs. Alexander Berger
Albert E. Bergin (In Memory of Alexina F. Bergin)
Herman Berkey
Mrs. Alice Berry
Mrs. F. Robert Bily
Mrs. Florence A. Bing
William Bischofberger
Mrs. Lewis S. Black
Blackman Plumbing Supply Company, Inc.
Dr. Julius B. Blankfein
Miss Hilda V. Blom
Pvt. Louis Blum Post No. 115,
 Jewish War Veterans of U. S. Inc.
†Colonel Marston T. Bogert
†Henry L. Bogert
†John L. Bogert
Harry Bohne
†Mrs. Anna Mary Bowne
†Miss Anellen Starr Bowne
†Miss Beatrice Bowne
†Ernest V. K. Bowne
†Harvey S. Bowne
†Herbert Sidney Bowne

---

†Bowne Descendant
*Deceased

†Miss Jean Bowne
†Miss Florence E. Bowne
†Thomas Burling Bowne
Mrs. William Broadwell Bowne
Otto H. Boysen
†Hugh Parsons Brady
G. A. Bramhall
Lieutenant Colonel Elmer H. Braun
Mrs. Clarence W. Brazer
Mrs. Charles H. Brigham
Richard H. Brown
†Peter Cooper Bryce
Reverend Archie Buchanan
Max Buehler
A. R. Butler
George F. Byrne
*Patrick Callan
Reverend Dr. Charles H. Campbell
Commander Carman Chapter, Daughters of the
 Union, 1861-1865, National Society, U. S.
John A. Cassidy
†Mrs. John J. Champieux
A. W. Chapman
E. J. Clark Carpet Company
Henry A. Clark, Jr.
William E. Code
Charles Cadwallader Colden
†Stephen W. Collins
†Harris Dunscombe Colt
Conovitz, Inc.
Honorable Joseph M. Conroy
Mrs. Helen Cookman
Milton L. Cornell
Cornucopia Lodge No. 563 F. and A. M.
*Mrs. Samuel A. Cox
†Mrs. Thomas Riggs Cox
Alfred D. Cummings
Irving G. Cummins
Miss Olga D. Dahlgren
Honorable Peter M. Daly
Mrs. Walter T. Daub
Daughters of American Revolution (Matinecock
 Chapter)
Daughters of 1812, National Society U. S. Treaty
 of Ghent Chapter
†Mrs. John S. Day
Mrs. Samuel R. Dayoff
Harry Dayton
*Hon. James A. Dayton
J. Wilson Dayton
Walter S. Dayton
Mrs. Sheldon W. Dean
Mrs. Zenobia De Jimenez
Honorable Alexander Del Giorno
Hugo E. DeMar

42

Regular Members (continued)

†Miss Odette H. de Mauriac
Mrs. Umberto de Novellis
†Francis Embree de Raismes
†W. Embree de Raismes
Miss Rae Dessell
Mrs. Isaac W. Diller
Dr. Mary Earhart Dillon
W. T. Dippel
Miss Helen Schuyler Dixon
†Mrs. Dorothy Tuckerman Draper
*Bruce R. Duncan
†Richard Bowne Durand

†Douglas L. Elliman
†Lawrence Bogert Elliman
†Dr. R. H. E. Elliott
†Miss Edith Franklin Embree
Exempt Firemen's Association of Flushing

Miss Julia M. Fanning
Mrs. Lillie T. Fanning
Donald F. Farabaugh
†Mrs. Louis D. Farnsworth, Sr.
Miss Edith P. Fetterolf
Mrs. W. Philip Fickett
*†Miss Margaret E. Field
†Dr. William H. Field
Paul B. Findley
Ernest B. Fischer
Miss Mildred A. Fitzgibbons
Flushing Chapter of Hadassah
Flushing Garden Club, Inc.
Flushing Monthly Meeting, Society of Friends
Flushing Progressive School
Flushing Window Cleaning, Inc.
Fox and Schamel, Inc.
†Miss Edna L. Franklin
†Dr. Lewis B. Franklin
†Mrs. Lewis B. Franklin
†Lindley Murray Franklin
†Miss Nina L. Franklin
Honorable Charles W. Froessel
†Mrs. R. W. Furman

*Mrs. S. Edson Gage
†Mrs. Frances C. W. Gardner
Mrs. Elsie Garner
Miss Sarah Louise Garner
Erwin Geissman
Mrs. Charlotte Gerstman
May F. Gerstman
†Mrs. Marion Bowne Gilbert
Wilbur E. Gilman
Alfred S. Githens
Frank L. Giusti
Paul F. Glasheen
John C. Glenn
†Mrs. Herbert Gnad
Dr. Benjamin Goldsmith

---

†Bowne Descendant
*Deceased

Good Citizenship League, Inc.
*†Mrs. Virginia Bowne Goodwin
†Mrs. J. Holdsworth Gordon, Jr.
Malcolm Montrose Graham
Miss Margaret A. Gram
Dr. Albert Griesbach

†Franklin M. Haines, Jr.
†Roland Bowne Haines
Reverend Dr. Norman A. Hall
*Howard L. Hallett
Eugene E. Halmos
E. Douglas Hamilton
*W. J. Hamilton
Walter T. Hanrahan
Douglas G. Hardgrove
*Seth W. Harpell
Mrs. Edith B. Harper
Earl S. Hartman
Frank P. Hayden
Mrs. Burton A. Hayner
Hebrew Women's Aid Society, Flushing Synagogue
Edmund Henninger
Alexander M. Hepburn
†Thomas Gaylord Herendeen
Henry G. Hillier
*Stuard Hirschman
Edward F. Hosinger
Mrs. Edna J. Hossfeld
George J. Hossfeld
†Mrs. Albert W. Humm
†Mrs. Theodore F. Humphrey
James Hunter, Jr.

C. E. Ising Corporation

†Miss Marion Jackson
Jamaica Veteran Volunteer Firemen's Association
†Dr. S. Ransom Jagger
Miss Corinne M. Jennings
Miss Gertrude F. Jennings
†Mrs. Dorothy Honeywell Johnston
H. Albert Johntra
*Mrs. J. Burnett Jones
Mrs. Samuel Day Jones

Mrs. George G. Kane, Jr.
Dr. Hans Kaufman
Mrs. Hugh T. Keating
*†Mrs. Louise N. Keese
†Miss Pauline S. Keese
Dr. Margaret V. Kiely
*Dr. Paul Klapper
Knickerbocker Ice and Coal Company
Mrs. W. W. Knowles
Franklin S. Koons
Miss Helen M. Kortlander
Reverend Detlef A. Kraft
Edwin V. Krolman
Harry Kurz

43

Regular Members (continued)

*Maurice A. Lahey
†Edward M. Lapham
†Mrs. Edward M. Lapham
Mrs. Louis B. Leggett
T. F. Leibfried
Frederick W. Lellé
Miss Abbie E. Lendrum
*Miss Emma Lendrum
William A. Leonard Post No. 422, American Legion, Inc.
†Edward A. LeRoy, Jr.
†John Minturn LeRoy
†Mrs. Katherine M. LeRoy
Milton S. Levinson
J. Howard Liberty
Lievendag Motors, Inc.
†Mrs. Ethel Bowne Licht
†Mrs. Alfred M. Longmere
†Mrs. Alfred F. Loomis
†Dr. May Murray Lowden
†Mrs. Thomas Baldwin Lowerre
Mrs. Robert P. Lowry
Clarence A. Ludlum
Mrs. James A. Lunn
Miss Agnes Lyall
Joseph P. Lynch

Gardiner L. Macey
†Mrs. Cuvier Lee MacGarr
Reverend Dougald Lachlan MacLean
Miss Mary MacLeod
†Miss Marion L. MacNab
Frank L. Maguth
Miss Ida Malcolm
Thomas F. Malone
Dr. Raymond Mandra
Manhasset First-Day School
Manhasset Preparative Meeting Religious Society of Friends
Louis Mantel
*†Mrs. Sarah Bowne Marsh
William Martens, Jr.
*Mrs. Everett P. Martin
Glenway Maxon
Miss Adele M. McCleary
Miss Hazel I. McCleary
Miss Margaret M. McCoon
Miss Sadie McCoon
Peter McDonald
K. V. McMillan
*Fred H. Mead
George W. Meier
Mrs. Ida A. Mellor
Dr. H. P. Mencken
Lester M. Mendell
Honorable Jesse Merritt
William Meyer
Irving Miller
†Henry Bedinger Mitchell
†J. F. B. Mitchell
†J. Macdonald Mitchell
†Miss Nina Cornelia Mitchell
Mrs. Harry E. Monk

†Rodman Bowne Montgomery
Mrs. Edward C. Moore
Mothers' Club of St. Andrew Avellino's Church
Nathaniel W. Murphy
†Eduard Mitchell Murray
John A. Murray, Jr.
National Council of Jewish Women, North Shore Section
National League of American Pen Women
Myron Neisloss
†William Bowne Nichols
Anthony J. Nittoli
Mrs. Gouverneur H. Nixon
Mrs. C. G. Noble
George F. Nolan
Miss Olivia J. Norris

†Dr. Mervin E. Oakes
Henry B. Oatley
Miss Anna M. O'Connor
Miss Marie T. O'Donnell
Frank S. O'Hara
Miss Florence O'Neill
Rabbi Charles Ozer

Miss Anna Pallem
*Dr. Victor Hugo Paltsits
Herman L. Papsdorf
Parent-Teachers Association of Flushing High School
Parent-Teachers Association of P. S. #20 (John Bowne School)
Mrs. Duncan Parham
Mrs. Rex Lee Paris
Mrs. Harold G. Parker
†Miss Mabel Bowne Parsons
†Reginald Bowne Parsons
John W. Pasta
†Mrs. O. Edward Payne
Herman I. Peck
S. H. P. Pell
Honorable Nicholas M. Pette
Honorable Alfred J. Phillips
E. W. Pittman
Mrs. August Plishker
Mrs. Joseph F. Poey
Charles U. Powell
Mrs. Charles U. Powell
†Mrs. George A. Post
John Prowse

†Murray T. Quigg
Hon. Samuel Rabin
William Rabkin
Reverend Dr. Alfred H. Rapp
Mrs. Alfred H. Rapp
Emile E. Rathgeber
Frederick S. Rauber
†Mrs. William T. Ray
Mrs. C. H. Reges
Mrs. Emma M. Rendall
Max Resnikoff
Dr. James R. Reuling
Herbert Ricard
*Honorable Rodman Richardson
Mrs. Charles H. Rickert
Dr. Otto C. Risch
*Arthur S. Ritter

---

†Bowne Descendant
*Deceased

Regular Members (continued)

Miss Constance Roberts
†Donald W. Roberts
†Miss Frances Bowne Roberts
Miss Gladys M. Roberts
Miss Mathilda Hoffman Roberts
Roberts Nash Construction Corporation
Mrs. Grace E. Roche
Mrs. Florence C. Rockefeller
Colonel James A. Roe
Mrs. James A. Roe
†Mrs. B. Pendleton Rogers
Miss Sabina Rogers
†Mrs. Rosalie Elliman Romeyne
Mrs. Jack Ross
Isaac Rothman
Mrs. Chester D. Rudolf

Lady Katherine R. Salvage
Mrs. John Sanders, Jr.
Mrs. Virginia Sandt
Mrs. Arthur Sard
Mrs. Thomas G. Schaedle
Leonard J. Schaefer
R. J. Schaefer
G. Schneider
Dr. Joseph C. Schreiner
Arthur Schulz
Otto Schulz
Henry T. Schwande
David L. Schwartz
Miss Marguerite A. Scott
Howard C. Sherwood
Elmer W. Silver
Mrs. Elmer W. Silver
Mrs. Watson Silver
Dr. E. D. Sinsabaugh
†Harry Bowne Skillman
Michael M. Skodnick
Miss Helen L. Slocum
*Frederick S. Sly
Mrs. Frederick S. Sly
Mrs. Jean E. Smalbach
Arthur R. Smith
Honorable Edward J. Smith
Mrs. L. C. L. Smith
William M. Smith
†Mrs. Eleanor A. Snell
†Mrs. Edgar Snipes
Louis Sobelson
Society for the Preservation of Long Island Antiquities
Sol Solway
†Mrs. Ruth Bowne Somerville
*Dr. Frederic Splint
*H. D. Springsteen
Mrs. Albert A. Staves
*Edward E. Stapleton
Starke, Cook and Ryan
Mrs. Reginald A. Steel
†Mrs. Frederick B. Stimson
S. Meredith Strong, Jr.
Russell F. Stryker
Mrs. Magdalen Sullivan
Sunrise Oil Company

*†Mrs. Rebecca Hyatt Sussdorf
†Effingham Bowne Sutton
Robert W. Swanson

†Mrs. Maud N. Talleur
*†Miss Anna C. Tatnall
†Edward C. Tatnall
John H. Tennent
Mrs. G. Kenneth Terrell
Dr. John J. Theobald
Dr. Joseph S. Thomas
Mrs. Jennie B. Thompson
†Rodman Tilt
†Mrs. Joseph B. Tisdale
†Mrs. William H. P. Townsend
†Benjamin H. Trask
Samuel S. Tripp
Giuseppe Trotta
Mrs. G. M. Tucker
†Mrs. Paul Tuckerman

†Miss Emma S. Underhill

Valentine Bros.
Arthur F. Van Dewater
Douglas Van Riper
†Mrs. John H. Vietor
Anthony Villett

Mrs. Sylvester Walker
*Mrs. William H. Walker
Mrs. Henry D. Waller
Mrs. Helen A. Walsh
Frederick H. Wappler
*Mrs. Frederick H. Wappler
Mrs. Edith M. Ward
George A. Ward
†Mrs. Alan Warner
†Mrs. Elizabeth Bowne Weelans
Charles J. Weidel
John Welsh
Mrs. John Welsh
Honorable Henry G. Wenzel, Jr.
†Mrs. Phebe S. Weston
Bernard Wexler
A. U. Whitson
Wigod's, Inc.
†Miss Eliza Keese Willets
Miss Eliza L. Willets
Mrs. Charles B. Williams
†Walter B. Williams
†Miss Mary Willis
Samson Winkler
Women's Club of Bayside, Inc.
Women's Guild, Church-on-the-Hill
Women's Republican Club of Flushing
Howell R. Wood
The Very Reverend Hubert S. Wood
†Mrs. John F. Wood
Lester W. Wright
Miss Nell E. Wright
Very Reverend Monsignor John D. Wynne

F. S. Yale
Mrs. William T. Yale
†Miss Mary F. Young
Victor A. Yorio

Mrs. Jerome Zwicker

†Bowne Descendant
*Deceased